LA CAZZARIA

*The Book
of the Prick*

LA CAZZARIA

The Book of the Prick

ANTONIO VIGNALI

EDITED AND TRANSLATED BY
IAN FREDERICK MOULTON

ROUTLEDGE
New York

Published in 2003 by
Routledge
29 West 35th Street
New York, NY 10001
www.routledge-ny.com

Copyright © 2003 by Taylor & Francis Books, Inc.

Routledge is an imprint of the Taylor & Francis Group.
Printed in the United States of America on acid-free paper.

10 9 8 7 6 5 4 3 2 1

Library of Congress Cataloging-in-Publication Data

Arsiccio, Intronato, 1500 or 1501–1559.
        [Cazzaria. English]
        La cazzaria: the book of the prick / by Antonio Vignali; edited and translated by Ian Frederick Moulton.
        p. cm.
        Includes bibliographical references and index.
        ISBN 0-415-94066-4 (alk. paper) — ISBN 0-415-94067-2 (pbk.: alk. paper)
        1. Arsiccio, Intronato, 1500 or 1501–1559. Cazzaria. I. Moulton, Ian Frederick, 1964– II. Title.

PQ4664. V63 C3913   2003
853'.3—dc21   2002031943

Contents

Editor's Acknowledgments

vii

Introduction
The Greatest Tangle of Pricks There Ever Was:
Knowledge, Sex, and Power in Renaissance Italy
IAN FREDERICK MOULTON

I

La Cazzaria (Siena, c. 1525)
ANTONIO VIGNALI

71

Bibliography

177

Editor's Acknowledgments

MY INTEREST IN *La cazzaria* developed over a period of several years, and was encouraged by many friends and colleagues. Pam Brown and Nancy Selleck invited me to speak on the subject at the Renaissance and Early Modern Colloquium at Princeton University in 1995. In that same year I presented a paper on Vignali as part of Mary Gallucci's panel on "Sodomy and Male Homosexuality" at the Sixteenth Century Studies conference in San Francisco. Peter C. Herman subsequently published my article on *La cazzaria* in his collection of essays honoring James Mirollo: *Opening the Borders: Inclusivity and Early Modern Studies* (University of Delaware Press, 1999).

At Routledge, my editors Emily Vail and Anne Davidson have been unfailingly helpful and supportive. A travel grant from Arizona State University West facilitated travel to Europe for primary research on *La cazzaria*, Siena, Vignali and the Intronati, and this book would have been impossible without the kind assistance of the staff at several libraries: the British Library, the Biblioteca

Nazionale Centrale in Florence, and above all the Biblioteca Communale in Siena. I am especially grateful to the Vatican Library for allowing me to study the Capponiano manuscript of *La cazzaria*. As always, the staff of Fletcher Library at Arizona State University West have been marvelous—especially the hard-working people at Inter-Library Loan.

I would like to thank Guido Ruggiero and Sasha Roberts for their friendship and hospitality. And I am grateful for the support of colleagues and friends in Phoenix, especially Dottie Broaddus, Duku Anokye, and Bob and Mary Bjork. Finally, this book would not have been written without Wendy Williams, who first encouraged me to undertake this project.

Introduction

The Greatest Tangle of Pricks There Ever Was: Knowledge, Sex, and Power in Renaissance Italy

Ian Frederick Moulton

No matter how ugly and vulgar a thing is, it is more
vulgar and ugly not to be knowledgeable about it.

—Arsiccio Intronato

It is a shame that Jorge Luis Borges seems never to have run across
La cazzaria. It is just the sort of impossibly odd text that lurks in
the shadows and footnotes of his intellectual fables. Though
Borges's natural modesty might have shrunk from *La cazzaria*'s juve-
nile obscenity, one suspects that the Spanish surrealists would have
delighted in it: Dalì and Picasso could have illustrated it. Buñuel
would have made it into a stunning film.

The similarity of *La cazzaria* to the work of the surrealists of
the 1930s is not accidental. Like Buñuel's *L'Age d'Or* or Dalì's
coprophilic and masturbatory paintings, *La cazzaria* is the product
of a hyper-intellectual, religiously skeptical, intensely masculine
community, and was written at a time when a traditional, deeply

Catholic society was undergoing massive social change and political disruption. Like Spain in the 1930s, Siena in the 1520s was a relatively open, democratic society threatened by internal military dictatorship and by the political domination of powerful neighboring states. In such troubling times, the response of intellectuals is often to turn inward to a world of art, fantasy, and play which promises imaginative freedom from unpleasant political realities. Buñuel, Dalì, and Lorca formed an informal society they called the Order of Toledo[1]; Antonio Vignali founded the very formal Accademia degli Intronati—the Academy of the Stunned.

One should not push such parallels too far—there are many significant differences between sixteenth-century Italy and twentieth-century Spain. But the similarities are useful because they help to explain and to situate *La cazzaria*, a text which in terms of Italian Renaissance culture can seem almost disturbingly unique.

I first encountered Antonio Vignali's *Cazzaria* in the North Reading Room of the old British Library in 1992. I was researching erotic writing in Renaissance England, and was searching for Italian texts, such as Aretino's *Dialogues*, which had influenced English writers. Until the early 1980s erotic texts in the British library had been kept in an area called the "Private Case" and had not been included in the General Catalogue.[2] By 1992 they were in the catalogue, and available to readers, though they had to be read at a special desk close to the librarians, so that they would not be used inappropriately. The bulk of material in the Private Case is made up of nineteenth- and early-twentieth-century texts, many bequeathed to the library in 1900 by Henry Spencer Ashbee, author of the Victorian erotic autobiography *My Secret Life*.

The edition of *La cazzaria* I came across was edited by Alcide

Bonneau and published by the firm of Lisieux in Paris in 1882. It was a French translation, with the original Italian on the facing pages, published in a limited edition of one hundred copies for collectors of erotic curiosities. The publisher, Isidore Lisieux, published a wide variety of erotic books, including similar editions of several other Italian Renaissance texts, including Aretino's *Sonetti lussuriosi* and *Ragionamenti*, and Lorenzo Venier's poem *La puttana errante*.

There is no shortage of erotic writing from sixteenth-century Europe, but nothing in my experience of early modern texts prepared me for *La cazzaria*. Aretino describes sex graphically, both in his sonnets and dialogues. Rabelais uses a carnivalesque language that revels in bodily functions, both sexual and digestive. Niccolò Franco and the writers of pasquinades employ shocking sexualized invective to attack their enemies. Like Aretino, *La cazzaria* is graphic, like Rabelais, it is carnivalesque, and it is full of polemical invective—but in both tone and content, it is unique.

For one thing, it is openly homoerotic, and its praise of sodomy, while often funny, is seldom ironic. It is clear that Arsiccio, the main character in the dialogue, very much prefers to have sex with men and is willing to openly assert and defend his preferences. In a society in which people were put to death for the crime of sodomy, such openness was both rare and dangerous.

The dialogue's title is deliberately rude and provocative: it comes from the Italian word *cazzo*, a slang term for "penis." For those interested in such details, it is pronounced "cazzarìa," not "cazzària," and ironically it is a feminine noun, as are many abstract nouns in the romance languages. The closest English rendering is probably "cockery"—but that is too close to "cookery" to be a useful translation. "Prickery" might work, but it lacks the specificity of the Italian word. In English, "prick" is a word with many meanings; in Italian *"cazzo"* can mean only one thing. In the text, I have translated *cazzo* as "cock," but "Book of the Cock" sounds like it might have something to do with poultry, so for the working English title, I settled on "Book of the Prick."

La cazzaria is a deeply paradoxical text: Although its vocabulary and concerns are crude it is nonetheless the product of a sophisticated academic culture. It is learned, but childish. It is at once mean-spirited and silly, bitter and whimsical. It is relentlessly masculine, unrelentingly sexual, deeply sexist, but not necessarily sexy.

In form, *La cazzaria* is a Platonic dialogue, an extremely popular genre in Renaissance Italy, especially for philosophical or didactic works such as Castiglione's *Book of the Courtier* and Bembo's *Asolani*. Like many other Italian Renaissance dialogues, *La cazzaria* begins with a frame tale that provides a fictional explanation of how the text came to be and presents it to prospective readers. The dialogue itself consists of a conversation between two young men, both actual members of the Accademia degli Intronati, a Sienese literary society. The men are referred to throughout by their academic pseudonyms, Arsiccio and Sodo. Arsiccio was the name taken by *La cazzaria*'s author, Antonio Vignali; Sodo was the academic name of Marcantonio Piccolomini, a close friend of Vignali's and a member of one of Siena's most prestigious families.

At the opening of the dialogue, Arsiccio, the older of the two men, is concerned that Sodo has made a fool of himself by showing himself ignorant of sexual matters in a conversation earlier in the evening. He offers to instruct Sodo about sex, and begins a lengthy discussion which deals with the nature and function of genital organs, the superiority of anal to vaginal sex, and various related topics. The text offers comic and facetious explanations of many bodily functions: why people fart when they are urinating; why genital organs smell and feel the way they do; why people kiss while having sex; why people have pubic hair.

Arsiccio is a secular scholar, and his social attitudes and opinions demonstrate a high level of hostility and even defensiveness. He is harshly critical both of the clergy, whom he sees as lustful hypocrites, and of common, uneducated people, whom he sees as clumsy and ignorant in sexual matters. He is also disdainful of women: he is frequently insulting in his references to female genitalia, and sees women as sexually voracious. Midway through the dialogue, Arsiccio recounts a fable in which a group of women complain to Jove that men's genitals are proportionally smaller than those of other male animals. Jove agrees to enlarge men's genitals on the condition that women consent to become like other female animals, which can mate only at certain times of the year. The women refuse. Another passage toys with the notion that women's vaginas were created when God removed material to make penises, a myth that Freud would have loved.

After a lengthy digression about the ignorance of those who don't read Latin and a debate over the nature and proper use of vernacular Italian, the second half of the dialogue is taken up with an extended fable of civic conflict in which personified body parts fight for dominance in an imaginary commonwealth. This tale of conflict between Cocks, Cunts, Assholes, and Balls is at once a commentary on the relationship between sexuality and power, and an allegory of contemporary Sienese politics in which the collapse of civic government is seen in terms of a torn and fragmented body. Each of the warring body parts corresponds to one of the major factions in the city. The tyrannical Cocks represent the dominant Monte dei Nove; the oppressed groups appear as Cunts, Balls, and Assholes. On one level, this allegory is obviously laughable and ridiculous. But it is also a deeply serious, even despairing analysis of social disintegration and civic collapse.

In *La cazzaria* Vignali radically rewrites philosophical notions dating to Greek and Roman antiquity that see the state as analogous to a human body: In this traditional view, the state is a body, ruled by a head (i.e., the ruling classes), in which each member, though unequal, does its part to work together to preserve the body's health. This way of seeing the state is clearly hierarchical and provides a powerful symbolic justification for social inequality. Even in contemporary democratic society, phrases like "head of state" or the use of the term "corporation" to refer to a group of people working together remain in our common speech as traces of these earlier conceptions of the "body politic."

In contrast to this classical model, in Vignali's text the body politic has no head—it is instead a site of endless struggle between various contending organs. While Vignali's political vision is more despairing than Machiavellian, he nonetheless shares Machiavelli's deeply secular view of political power. *La cazzaria* ultimately sees social struggle as a struggle for sexual power and pleasure, as various discontented members come together to take power away from the phallic ruling class. Their revolt, however, is inconclusive and the newly empowered factions immediately squabble among themselves. At the time Vignali was writing, Siena was one of the few Italian city-states to retain a republican government and the city's independence was under threat from its more powerful neighbors. It is no coincidence that Vignali, like his contemporary Machiavelli, sees factionalism and civic disunity as a major threat to the survival of an independent state.

After bringing his political allegory to a close, Arsiccio finally answers the question Sodo could not: why the balls do not enter either the cunt or the asshole during sex. The dialogue ends with Arsiccio and Sodo in Arsiccio's bed drinking wine, and it is strongly hinted that, having initiated Sodo into the realms of sexual knowledge, Arsiccio will sodomize him as well.

La cazzaria was written for circulation among an educated male elite, and its prejudices and biases are those of that elite. The relentless misogyny of *La cazzaria* is shared by other contemporary erotic texts written by upper-class men, such as Lorenzo Venier's poems *La puttana errante* and *La trentuna di Zaffetta*. The use of sexualized language in invective was common both in sixteenth-century satire and also—perhaps surprisingly—in university disputations. The sexual explicitness of Vignali's text is matched both by the anonymous pasquinades circulated in Rome, and by Niccolò Franco's sonnets from *Priapia* and the *Rime contra Aretino*. And the stories of sodomitical monks and sexually insatiable housewives in the first part of the dialogue were commonplaces of humanist culture—some are modeled on the *Facetiae*, Bracciolini's Latin collection of jests; others go all the way back to the second century and Apulieus's *The Golden Ass*.

Its humanist and academic origins ensure that *La cazzaria* differs greatly from the other great erotic dialogue from sixteenth-century Italy: Aretino's *Ragionamenti* (*Dialogues*). Aretino recounts erotic conversations between lower-class women, not educated men. And where Vignali praises scholars, Aretino is scornful of intellectuals; his *Dialogues* often show sympathy with servants and prostitutes rather than with their masters. Vignali's dialogue also differs from Aretino's in his outspoken praise of sex between men. Even though Aretino himself had sexual relations with men, his erotic writing never openly advocates homoerotic activity the way that Vignali's does, and the sex described in the *Dialogues* is mostly between men and women.

La cazzaria was published in several editions within five or ten years of its composition—almost certainly without Vignali's consent. The dialogue was fairly well-known in the sixteenth century, though it was suppressed by the Counter-Reformation Church and has largely been neglected since. Given recent scholarly interest in the historical relations between sexuality, knowledge, and power, an English language edition of Vignali's dialogue is long overdue. A humanist text that is also explicitly homoerotic, *La cazzaria* is an important document for the history of homosexuality and for the history of sexuality in general. It raises crucial issues about the relations between politics, sexuality, and the pursuit of knowledge and it demonstrates how intimately erotic and political discourses were linked in early modern Italy.

SOCIAL AND POLITICAL CONTEXTS

Although its explicit language and outspoken sexuality may seem quite modern, *La cazzaria* is topical text that is closely tied to the time and place of its composition. The dialogue is very much a product of 1520s Siena, a central Italian city-state with a population of about nineteen thousand at the time of the dialogue's composition.[3] Siena had been an independent republic since the early twelfth century, but in the early sixteenth century the city was entering into a period of political crisis that would ultimately result in the collapse of the state and the loss of its independence. The contemporary crisis of the Sienese republic is fundamental to *La cazzaria*'s exploration of the relations between sexuality and power.

Political instability in the period was by no means restricted to Siena. Before the 1490s, Italian politics was dominated by five major states: Milan, Venice, Florence, Naples, and the Papal States. The relations between these states were characterized by commercial rivalry and frequent though indecisive military activity; until 1494 they and their smaller neighbors like Siena, Mantua, and Ferrara maintained a precarious balance of power. In that year, however, Charles VIII of France invaded the peninsula in order to assert his claim to the crown of Naples. Though ultimately unsuccessful, his invasion demonstrated the clear inferiority of Italian mercenary troops to the national armies of the European dynastic states. From this point on, the independent Italian city-states found themselves under increasing political and military pressure from larger foreign powers. For the next fifty years, the peninsula became a battleground for the conflict between the Valois of France and the Hapsburgs, who after 1519 ruled both Spain and the Holy Roman Empire. Milan was conquered first by the French, then by the Spanish; Naples and Florence eventually came under Hapsburg control. Papal Rome was sacked in 1527 by Imperial troops. Only Venice managed to maintain its independence—but it emerged from the struggle a permanently weakened minor power. In such circumstances, independent Siena didn't stand a chance.

To make matters worse, Siena was internally divided into squabbling factions known as *monti*. Each of the five *monti* represented groups of families that had constituted the governing class of the city at various periods. The first to be formed was the

Gentilhuomini (Gentlemen), who ruled the city in the twelfth century. They represented the old feudal nobility and included great landowning families such as the Piccolomini and the Tolomei. The second was the Monte dei Nove (the Nine) made up of patricians—bankers, wealthy merchants, cloth magnates—who ruled the city during its period of greatest power and prestige in the late thirteenth and early fourteenth centuries. The Dodici (the Twelve) were the guildsmen who seized power from the Nove in 1355. The Riformatori (Reformers) took power in 1368. They and the final *monte*, the Popolari (the People) were made up primarily of shopkeepers and artisans.[4] Although over half of all Sienese were not affiliated with any *monte* and were thus excluded from the political process, Siena had a government more broadly representative than any other contemporary Italian civic republic its size.

While each of the *monti* had originally represented a particular social and economic group, by the sixteenth century they had become hereditary associations of citizens, who were brought together by their families' historic membership in the group, rather than by class, occupation, wealth, or geography.[5] Economic and social divisions in the city-state thus cut across party lines, and each group contained both wealthy and poor members from various social groups.

In the early sixteenth century, the government of the city was largely in the hands of the Monte dei Nove, who sought to establish an oligarchy by taking as much power to themselves as possible. The Nove were opposed primarily by the Popolari and the Riformatori, who sought to widen popular participation in civic government, partly so that they might increase their own power. The factional disputes within Siena reflected the larger struggles in Italy as a whole. The Nove sided with Florence, the Medici papacy, and the French; the other parties with the Hapsburg emperor Charles V. In supporting the Florentines and the pope, the Nove found themselves on the wrong side of Sienese history, for the city had traditionally been pro-Imperial and for centuries Sienese politics had been defined by the city's rivalry with Florence, its more powerful northern neighbor.

Before the 1490s, Sienese civic government had by and large avoided falling into the hands of one man or family, as happened in many other Italian city-states. In the early years of the sixteenth century, however, power became increasingly consolidated in the person of Pandolfo Petrucci, leader of the Nove.[6] Assisted by his shrewd counsellor, Antonio da Venafro, Pandolfo dominated the Balìa, the Sienese elected assembly. He consolidated his power by assassinating his main rivals, including Niccolò Borghesi, his own father-in-law. Pandolfo's opposition to the ambitions of Cesare Borgia forced him to flee the city temporarily in early 1502, but he was quickly restored by the French, and his hold on power became even firmer after Cesare's death in 1507.[7]

Following Pandolfo's own death in 1512, power ultimately passed to his youngest son, Fabio, who attempted to strengthen his position by taking power away from other members of the Nove. These excluded members joined with members of other groups— the Monte del Popolo and the Riformatori—to overthrow Fabio in September 1524. Getting rid of Fabio was easy; deciding what to do next was not. The excluded members of the Nove wanted to reestablish an oligarchy with themselves at its head. The Popolari, Riformatori, and other groups wanted a return to a more inclusive communal government that involved all parties.

After the fall of Fabio's government, the Nove worked to con-
solidate civic power in the hands of another of their members,
Alessandro Bichi. But on 6 April 1525, following news of the dev-
astating defeat of the Nove's French allies at the battle of Pavia,
Bichi was assassinated by the Popolari. After Bichi's death the
other leaders of the Nove were banished from the city. They fled
to Florence and led an attack on the city by the Florentine and
Papal forces, which was defeated at the battle of Camollia on 25
July 1526. One year later, on 26 July 1527, the entire Monte dei
Nove were formally stripped of their civic rights. Soon afterward,
Imperial troops occupied the city. Although Siena remained nom-
inally independent for another thirty years, it had clearly become
a puppet state of the Hapsburgs. *La cazzaria* is thus a product of
the turbulent period of the republic's collapse. It chronicles the
death of Sienese independence, both in Arsiccio's allegorical fable
and in its general pessimism about worldly affairs.

Antonio Vignali and the Academy of the Intronati

Just as *La cazzaria* reflects a particular political moment, it is also the
product of a specific social and intellectual environment. In 1525,
after Fabio Petrucci had been driven from power, a young nobleman
named Antonio Vignali and five of his friends agreed to form a
group to promote the study of the liberal arts. Jacopo Antonio
Piero Vignali di Buonaggionti, author of *La cazzaria*, was born in
Siena in late 1500—there is a record of his baptism on 11
November of that year.[8] Although Vignali was clearly not one of
Fabio's supporters, his family was part of the politically dominant
Monte dei Nove, and was long established in the city. The
Buonaggionti Vignali first appear in the Sienese records in 1370, as

cloth merchants. The family was still prominent in Antonio Vignali's time, and his father, Alessandro, served as *gonfaloniere* for the Sienese *terza* (or neighborhood) of Camollia in both 1510 and 1512.

Vignali seems to have been one of the leading intellectual figures of Siena in the 1520s, but little is known of his personal life. One seventeenth-century account claims that he was "almost a monster because of his deformed body," but if this was the case it is not clear what the nature of his deformity was, or if he was deformed from birth. When choosing an academic pseudonym, Vignali chose "Arsiccio" or "burned." Perhaps the name was an ironic reference to his "monstrous" appearance, though it might also have jokingly been intended to suggest he was consumed by passion.

The founding of the Accademia degli Intronati is first recorded in a Latin letter written by Mino Celsi, a Sienese contemporary of Vignali's, to a friar named Betto Romano. Celsi writes that, "In the year 1525, six Sienese noblemen, to promote poetry and eloquence in the Tuscan, Latin and Greek languages founded a society for reading, interpreting, writing, and debating, to which they gave the name of Intronati."[9]

A fuller account of the Academy's founding can be found in Guido Pancirolo's *De claris legum interpretibus* (1637)—the same source that suggests Vignali was deformed:

> Four young men of the best character from our city, Arsicium,
> Sodum, Masconertum and Flavum, were students of law [in Pisa];
> but they were less given to legal study than to the zealous pursuit
> of more refined literature, and they studied the poems of
> Francisco Petrarch privately amongst themselves. Arsiccio, the pri-
> mary instigator, was accounted almost a monster because of his

deformed body, but nevertheless he had a brilliant spirit, however badly housed. Their teacher often maintained, reproaching them, that they made themselves "intronatos," since they found few auditors—this was the name the Sienese used for the deaf. Turning this into a joke, they began in turn to call themselves "intronatos." After they returned to Siena, they joined with other men of sharp wit, and instituted the famous Academy of this name.[10]

While accounts of the founding of the Academy differ,[11] all sources agree that Vignali was instrumental in bringing the group together. Besides Vignali (Arsiccio) and Marcantonio Piccolomini (Sodo), the other founders of the Academy are thought to have been Archbishop Francesco Bandini Piccolomini (Scaltrito), Francesco Sozzi (Importuno), Giovan Francesco Franceschi (Moscone or Masconertum), and Alessandro Marzi (Cirloso or Flavum). In the official register of the Academy's members in the Biblioteca Comunale in Siena these six names all appear in sequence, beginning with Scaltrito. A marginal note in the same hand as the entries states, "Here truly begin the Intronati."[12] The previous names in the list refer not to the Academy founded in 1525 but to its fifteenth-century precursor, the Accademia Grande.

The prologue to the Academy's constitution, probably written in the mid-sixteenth century, describes the Academy's purpose in the florid rhetoric typical of such documents:

In that time when barbarian arms, attracted by the discord of our states from the farthest regions of the West, invaded the sacred house of God and banished all thoughts but those of war not only from Tuscany, but from all of Italy, and disrupted and ruined all intellectual activity, in our city a few noble spirits of diverse

quality and accomplished learning—for many and diverse reasons
herein described—decided to form a group in which, as much as
the strength of their wits would allow, putting aside all distracting,
troublesome thoughts and all worldly cares, with sole and firm
intent devoted themselves to the pursuit of letters, in the vernacular as well as in Greek and Latin, reading, debating, gathering,
interpreting, writing, and to sum up, doing all they could. It was
not only a school of philosophy, but of humanities, law, music,
poetry, arithmetic, and universally of all the disciplines and all the
liberal and noble arts. . . . And since it was their intention to pay
no attention and give no care to any other thing in the world, it
pleased them to call themselves the Intronati.[13]

In this account, the name, Intronati, does not suggest "deaf"
or "foolish" so much as "beaten up." Assaulted by the invasions
and political upheavals of Italy in the 1520s, the Intronati are
numb to the external world. Like a character in a cartoon who hal-
lucinates after being hit on the head, they turned from the violence
of the world around them into a world of fantasy. The Academy's
motto attests to the wariness of its founders and their desire to
construct a haven of playful scholarship in a harsh world: *Orare,
Studere, Gaudere, Neminem laedere, Nemini credere, De mundo non curare*
(Pray, Study, Rejoice, Harm no one, Believe no one, Have no care
for the world).[14] The same cautious tone is echoed in *La cazzaria*
when Arsiccio warns Sodo that "these are uncertain times and
things rarely work out as planned"(116).

Groups of literary men like the Intronati were inspired to a
certain extent by the humanist societies active in Rome and
Florence in the late fifteenth century—especially the Roman
Academy founded by Pomponio Leto and the Platonic Academy

of Marsilio Ficino.[15] These groups, devoted to the rediscovery of the literature of classical antiquity, attracted many of the greatest Italian scholars of the time. Poliziano, Cristofero Landino, and Pico della Mirandola were all associated with Ficino's Academy. Meetings of the Roman Academy were attended by Paolo Giovio, Baldassare Castiglione, and Pietro Bembo, among others.

But along with this heritage of serious scholarship and debate, academies like the Intronati also had a more lighthearted model: groups like Poggio Bracciolini's Bugiale, or Liars' Club, in which highly educated, culturally sophisticated men gathered to amuse themselves with jokes and bawdy tales. Bracciolini (1380–1449) was a Florentine humanist who spent over fifty years as a papal secretary and published a Latin collection of jests, called the *Facetiae*. According to Bracciolini, the Bugiale functioned as a forum for humor, but also for serious criticism and political debate which could not be expressed in other places. Its meetings were characterized by jests and invective, and gave papal courtiers a chance to blow off steam:

> Until the reign of Pope Martin we were in the habit of selecting, within the precincts of the court, a secluded room where we collected the news of the day, and conversed on various subjects, mostly with a view to relaxation, but also with serious intent. There no one was spared, and we freely attacked whomever or whatever met with our disapproval; often the Pope himself was the subject of our criticism.[16]

Academies like the Intronati provided a similar opportunity for scholars and courtiers to express themselves in a closed group that encouraged criticism and disputation.

In many ways these academies functioned as an alternative to traditional universities. The University of Siena, a flourishing institution strongly supported by all factions in the city, focused primarily on legal studies and—like all universities—conducted its business in Latin.[17] In contrast to the classical preoccupations of Leto's and Ficino's groups, sixteenth-century academies like the Intronati rejected the Latin of the universities and focused instead on literary production and intellectual debate in the vernacular.[18] It is typical of *La cazzaria's* academic origins that Vignali chose to write in Italian and not Latin.

The Intronati was one of the first of the new academies to be established, and it arguably had a major influence on the development of similar groups in other cities. Like later Italian academies, the Intronati used symbolic or satiric pseudonyms for their members, and had a detailed system of rules and officials governing the group's activities. The group met every Sunday to discuss writing produced by its members. It was led by an officer called an Archintronato who was elected for a term of two months. He had two assistants, called *consiglieri,* who could conduct business in his absence. There were also six *censori* who would review members' compositions before the meeting in order to "correct" and "polish" their grammar and style. In addition, a *cancelliere* would keep minutes of meetings and maintain files of works submitted to the group. A *tesoriere* kept track of the finances.[19] The democratic and participatory governing structure of the Academy kept alive notions and structures of Republican governance at a time when civic government throughout Italy was becoming increasingly despotic.

The intellectual idealism embodied in the Intronati is evident at several points in *La cazzaria.* For all its clever ironies, Vignali's dialogue is quite earnest about the intrinsic value of learning.

Arsiccio insists that intellectual pursuits should not be driven by the desire for gain: "If anyone devotes himself to study because he needs to earn his bread, you know he will never achieve anything worthwhile, because study should be a delight and not a necessity. Otherwise he will never seek to know more than what he needs to get some little thing he wants; and thus from the very outset, knowledge is parted from learning" (118–19). Like scholars of all periods, Arsiccio is pessimistic about the state of education: he laments that "the clever and subtle things in which we are wiser than the ancients all have to do with making money, dominating others, and similar things; and all depends on this, because wealth has placed its feet on virtue's neck" (119).

Arsiccio's notions of proper education follow a humanist model: education must be broad, and it must be useful. Like Castiglione's courtier, Arsiccio's ideal pupil should be at ease in any social situation: "Clearly it is better to know many things than to be very learned in only one area, for these days you often find yourself among diverse people, who have diverse abilities." But the advice continues in a franker vein than anything in *The Courtier*: "you have to talk now of law, now of love, now of philosophy, now of buggery, now of fucking, now of one thing and another" (81). Passages like this are remarkable for their open acceptance of sexual relations as an integral part of everyday human existence—a point of view which Vignali's dialogue shares with both Aretino and Boccaccio.

After their founding in 1525, the Intronati quickly became prominent in Sienese cultural life. Their primary focus was the promotion of vernacular literature, especially drama. As Vignali's digression on language in *La cazzaria* suggests, like many sixteenth-century Italian intellectuals, the Intronati were involved in debates

over the proper form of Italian. Their most enduring literary mon-
ument was the 1532 comedy *Gl'Ingannati* (The Deceived), a tale of
mistaken identity whose cross-dressed heroine proved quite influential: Shakespeare drew heavily on the play, directly or indirectly,
for the plot of *Twelfth Night*. Besides *Gl'Ingannati*, the members of
the Academy wrote several other successful plays, and a collection
of the Academy's plays, many by Alessandro Piccolomini, was
published in 1611. Though it was periodically closed for political
reasons, the academy Vignali founded lasted for over two hundred
years, and today the library of the Intronati forms the basis of the
collection of the Sienese Civic Library, the Biblioteca Communale.

In 1527, following the Sack of Rome and political defeat of
the Nove, Siena fell more and more under the control of Imperial
forces. Vignali's family seems to have been going through difficult
times as well; that same year, Vignali's father, Alessandro, was
accused of murder, though the charges were soon dropped by
order of the Sienese Balìa, suggesting either that he was innocent,
or—perhaps more likely—that he enjoyed a high level of political
protection.[20] By the early 1530s, Imperial troops occupied Siena
and Emperor Charles V became the ultimate arbiter of the city's
politics. Though Antonio Vignali's family does not figure in the
lists of those banished, he chose to leave Siena around this time.
He was thus no longer in the city in 1532 when the Intronati
wrote *Gl'Ingannati*, although the play incorporates idiomatic expres-
sions used in *La cazzaria*. The Sienese republic continued in name
until the 1550s, when it was finally conquered by the Medici
dukes of Florence, who by that time were also allies of the
emperor. It seems that by that time Vignali's family welcomed the
republic's collapse. Two of Vignali's brothers, Giovan Battista and

Gismondo, were executed on 13 June 1553 for attempting to betray the city to the Imperial forces.[21]

Vignali's own politics are somewhat unclear, as are his reasons for leaving the city. After his departure from Siena, Vignali seems to have wandered around western Europe, finding employment as a secretary at the courts of various nobles. Perhaps the most complete early account of his life is found in Isidoro Ugurgieri-Azzolini's *Le pompe sanesi* (Pistoia, 1649), a compendium of biographical sketches of illustrious citizens of Siena. There Vignali is described as something of a rebel; a man of "elevated intelligence and most vivacious spirits, not suitable to the humor of those who, in his day, were more powerful in the Republic than he was" (575–76). He is said to have loved his city, and left it voluntarily at a time when he could foresee that its independence was doomed. After leaving Siena, he traveled through Spain, France, and other parts of Italy and Germany, "leaving everywhere signs of his worth." Ugurgieri-Azzolini and others report that during his travels Vignali served the future Philip II of Spain, an odd choice of patron, if he did indeed leave Siena because he resented the Imperial hegemony. At any rate, in 1540–1541 Vignali was in Seville, for a letter survives which he wrote to a certain Camilla Saracini from there on 20 March 1541, sending her his translation of the eleventh book of the *Aeneid*.[22] Camilla Saracini belonged to an established Sienese family with whom the Vignalis seem to have been connected; a Pierfrancesco Saracini was pardoned in connection with the same murder as Vignali's father.

Ugurgieri-Azzolini attests that Vignali died in Milan in April 1559 at the age of fifty-eight, while in the service of Cardinal Cristofero Madruzzi, and that he was buried in the monastic church of San Bernardino. *Le pompe sanesi* also records Vignali's epitaph, which suggests that he and Marcantonio Piccolomini, his imagined interlocutor from *La cazzaria*, remained close friends:[23]

> Whoever you are, if you are devout, do not hold back your devoted tears. Here lies Antonio Vignali, Arsiccio Intronato, Citizen of Siena, a man of sharp and admirable wit, dedicated above all to letters, painting, and the plastic arts. He was exceedingly well-disposed to such pleasing trifles. He lived fifty-eight years, four months, and thirteen days, and died six days before the Nones of April, 1559, with his companion from Petra to Mauritius, Senator and Bishop of Vigevano, his dearest friend Senator Marcantonio Piccolomini himself, his closest colleague, attending and following. It is difficult to determine who is sadder—the one dead, or the other living.

While commemorating Vignali's friendship with Piccolomini, this epitaph does not mention that Vignali was married, though it seems that he must have been, for two sons of his, Curzio and Ciro, are mentioned in legal papers dating from 1555.[24] Scipione Bargagli's 1602 dialogue *Il Turamino, overro del parlare e dello scritto sanese* (Turamino, or On Sienese Speech and Writing) features Curzio Vignali as one of its interlocutors. The characters in the dialogue all speak well of Curzio's father, Antonio (though they never mention *La cazzaria*), and there is no suggestion that Curzio is illegitimate.[25] No mention is made of his mother though, neither here nor in any other account of Vignali's life.

LA CAZZARIA AS AN ACADEMIC TEXT

As we have seen, *La cazzaria* was one of the first intellectual products of the Intronati, and the dialogue's academic origins are apparent at every point.[26] Both speakers in the dialogue, and many of the people they refer to are members of the Intronati. All are referred to by their academic pseudonyms, and there seem to be a fair number of in-jokes that cannot be fully understood by readers outside the Academy. In the fictional frame introducing the text, one of the Intronati finds the document in Vignali's rooms and secretly borrows it to share with the group's leader, the Archintronato. Although fictional, this story may have been prophetic. It is inconceivable that Vignali would have sanctioned the printing of a text as provocative and offensive as *La cazzaria*, and at some point, whether through friends or enemies, it must have gotten out of his control and into the hands of a printer. In any case, all indications are that the dialogue was intended primarily for manuscript circulation among members of the Academy.

Just as academies formed an informal and even playful alternative to universities, so *La cazzaria* mocks the form and content of intellectual discourse. As we have seen, the dialogue form itself is typical of serious sixteenth-century texts. And as in many scholarly Latin texts, the discussion in Vignali's dialogue is divided into a series of *quaestiones*, which appear in the margins of the earliest editions.[27] This method of structuring a text is typical of a medieval Scholasticism which by Vignali's time was coming to seem stuffy and outdated. Some of the *quaestiones* in *La cazzaria* are identical to those found in serious academic texts: "Why Learning has been Abandoned"; "Why Classical Philosophers Hated Wealth"; and "Why Latin Works are Translated into the Vernacular." But most of them are ridiculous and bawdy parodies: "Why Women's Asses Have No Hair"; "Why We Kiss with the Tongue when Fucking"; and "Why, as Soon as Man Has Shit, He Looks at the Turd."

La cazzaria mocks intellectual methods and modes of argumentation by applying them to sexual and bodily knowledge. Since the time of Plato, Western philosophical thought has sought to elevate itself by stressing a distinction between the mind and body. The mind is the gateway to spirituality and higher truth, the body the seat of base material pleasures and sensual illusion. Arsiccio's parodic discourse is based on the proposition that the two realms are in fact linked, because the mind is part of the body. If scholars are serious in their desire to study the natural world, Arsiccio says, then they should devote their attentions to genitalia, human reproduction, and sexual pleasure: As he explains to Sodo early in the dialogue, "Since knowledge of the secrets of nature brings glory, honor, and reputation, it ought to be glorious and praiseworthy to seek out the secrets of the cunt, especially considering the great care wise Nature took in making her to be the mold and habitation of such a noble animal as man" (85). Although intellectuals often like to pretend their philosophical musings are detached from the material and physical realities of life, Arsiccio insists that there is no way to separate the intellectual from the sexual. In Renaissance universities (as in modern ones) the walls and students' benches are covered not with philosophic propositions but with sexual graffiti, and in *La cazzaria* fucking and buggery are described as academic specialties, just like law and philosophy. Arsiccio's privileging of the lower body at the expense of the upper is comically epitomized in his description of a person getting out of bed: "most people, when they get up in the morning, the first thing they do is put their ass where their head has lain all night, as a sign that in matters of honor and reverence the head gives way to the ass, because the ass is a worthier and nobler part of the body" (94).

Besides reversing the traditional hierarchy which sees the head as superior to the lower parts of the body, in *La cazzaria* Arsiccio subordinates "higher" intellectual skills to the lower body by devoting all his scholarship to knowledge of sexual pleasure and bodily functions. In the fictional letter prefacing the dialogue, Arsiccio is praised for having "discovered all the causes and circumstances of fucking" (74), language which recalls Aristotelian logic and its hair-splitting distinctions between various sort of causes for events. Similarly, Arsiccio offers to explain to Sodo, through mock-Scholastic reasoning, why it is clear that cocks are made of matter. He later argues facetiously that the asshole is the most valued part of the body—why else is buggery punished more harshly than any other form of assault? These ridiculous and topsy-turvy arguments make fun of Scholastic logic as well as mocking the tradition of argumentation *pro et contra* in which students were required to write elaborate discourses on both sides of seemingly pointless questions such as "Is Day Better than Night?" or "Does Learning Make Men Happier than Ignorance?"

Arsiccio's mocking rejection of the Scholastic past is matched by his valorization of experience and observation over academic tradition and received opinion: He admits that sexual matters "are not found . . . in the works of any ancient or modern authority, but nonetheless the cock, the cunt, and the asshole are things that are handled and used every day. It does not seem credible that anyone could be so foolish not to understand this for himself" (82).

Despite Arsiccio's praise of experience and common sense, *La cazzaria* is outspoken in its disdain for the uneducated. Arsiccio insists that students and academics make better lovers of women than laborers or the unlearned, not only because they speak so eloquently, but also because they are discreet, and know when to be silent. They also, according to Arsiccio, know effective methods of contraception and can supply abortifacients. However attractive Arsiccio's arguments on this point may have been to his academic audience, his claims are somewhat exaggerated: Contraceptive lore, especially knowledge of which herbs could induce abortion, was the province of midwives, not scholars.[28] And although sodomy and sexual license were frequently associated with the educated and the social elite, in Renaissance Florence, at least, sodomitical relationships were found at all social levels.[29] Even Arsiccio's blithe assertion that the learned are more sexually skilled than the common people was a contentious point in the erotic literature of the period. In Aretino's *Dialogues*, Nanna the courtesan gives the opposite view, complaining at length about the perversions of the learned and asserting that common people make much better lovers.[30]

La cazzaria's elitism comes out most strongly in its concern with the power of language—both in the passages of political oratory in which the various parts of the body speak out, but also in the one section of the dialogue that does not deal with erotics: a discussion of the proper use of the Tuscan language. Questions of language aroused intense scholarly debate in sixteenth-century Italy. On the one hand, as was the case all over Europe, intellectual discourse was shifting from Latin to the vernacular. Machiavelli, Bembo, and Castiglione all wrote in Italian. But in Italy the problem of the vernacular was complicated both by the variety of regional dialects, and—ironically—by Italy's distinguished vernacular literary tradition. Unlike England and France, which were dominated by capital cities whose dialects evolved into the official national language, Italy was a patchwork of competing city-states. For a variety of reasons Tuscan, the language of Florence, ended up as the basis for modern standard Italian, but in the sixteenth century Tuscan linguistic dominance was by no means assured. Besides debates over whether an author should write in Tuscan or his native dialect, there were also disputes over which variety of Tuscan one should use: the present language defined by common daily usage, or the archaic Tuscan of the great fourteenth-century authors Dante, Boccaccio, and Petrarch.

While scholars such as Benedetto Varchi argued in favor of modern Tuscan usage, in *La cazzaria* Arsiccio, following Pietro Bembo, takes a more conservative and elitist approach. He contends that common people cannot understand even the beauties of their own vulgar tongue because they do not understand the Latin out of which it evolved. He tells Sodo that he plans to write his magnum opus, *Lumen pudendorem* (The Light of Shame), in Latin so that only the learned will understand it. Ironically, Arsiccio's elitist conservatism is undercut by Vignali's own career: Not only is *La cazzaria* itself in Italian, but several years later Vignali also translated two books of Virgil into Tuscan—an activity Arsiccio explicitly condemns.

POLITICAL ALLEGORY IN *LA CAZZARIA*

Although the ridiculous obscenity of Vignali's text seems to amply fulfill the Academy's injunction to "have no care for the world," his political allegory representing the struggle for civic power in Siena in terms of a conflict between bodily organs is both sophisticated and topical. The metaphor of the city or commonwealth as a body is an ancient one, and in most cases the comparison functions to stress the naturalness of established structures of social and political power. Perhaps the most famous classical example is the fable of the belly said to have been told by the patrician Menenius Agrippa to calm the rebellious citizens of republican Rome. In its earliest recorded form, the story is told by Livy as follows: Many years ago, in a time of civic strife between plebeians and patricians, an emissary of the patricians went to speak to the people and dissuade them from rebellion:

> Menenius Agrippa, an eloquent man . . . simply told [the plebeians] the following fable in primitive and uncouth fashion. "In the days when all the parts of the human body were not as now agreeing together, but each member took its own course and spoke its own speech, the other members, indignant at seeing that everything acquired by their own care and labor and ministry went to the belly, whilst it, undisturbed in the middle of them all, did nothing but enjoy the pleasures provided for it, entered into a conspiracy; the hands were not to bring food to the mouth, the mouth was not to accept it when offered, the teeth were not to masticate it. Whilst, in their resentment, they were anxious to coerce the belly by starving it, the members themselves wasted away, and the whole body was reduced to the last stage of exhaustion. Then it became evident that the belly rendered no idle service, and the nourishment it received was no greater than that which it bestowed by returning to all parts of the body this blood by which we live and are strong. . . ." By using this comparison, and showing how the internal disaffection amongst the parts of the body resembled the animosity of the plebeians against the patricians, he succeeded in winning over his audience. Negotiations were then entered upon for a reconciliation.
>
> (Livy, *Ad urbe condita* 2.32–2.33)[31]

The moral of Menenius's fable is self-evident: in a healthy body, as in a healthy city, all parts work harmoniously at their different tasks. The indolent belly is as necessary as the industrious hands; the filthy anus (to carry the analogy a step further) is as crucial to healthy function as the delicate mouth.

The harmony of such a body is accentuated by the elision of the most contentious question raised by the allegory of the body politic—who is to be head and rule the body? By imagining ruler-ship not as rational direction by a superior head but as simple distribution of goods and services by the centrally located belly, Menenius's analogy avoids important questions of social hierarchy.

Menenius's fable of the belly, recounted by Livy and Plutarch and eventually dramatized by Shakespeare in *Coriolanus*,[32] was well-known in early modern Europe. In his *Defense of Poesy* (1595), Sir Philip Sidney attested that Menenius's story was well known and marveled at the calming and pacifying effect the patrician tale had on its plebeian listeners. "This [tale] applied by [Menenius] wrought such effect in the people, as I never read that ever words brought forth but then so suddaine and good an alteration, for upon reasonable conditions a perfect reconcilement ensued."[33] Perfect reconcilement may be characteristic of a healthy civic body, but as we have seen, Siena in the 1520s was not a healthy body. It was, one might say, a monstrous body. In *La cazzaria*, the body politic is fragmented—a collection of warring parts.

The notion of the body politic is one that has received an enormous amount of critical attention from literary critics and the-orists, traditional historians, and new historicists. As a trope it is so familiar as to be unremarkable—one refers quite unconsciously to "heads of state," "deliberative bodies," and "corporations"—and yet it remains a strikingly radical and alien notion for modern and postmodern readers who tend to perceive power as being disembodied and government as impersonal and bureaucratic. Take, for example, Michel Foucault's influential formulation:

> Power must be understood in the first instance as the multiplicity
> of force relations immanent in the sphere in which they operate
> and which constitute their own organization; as the process which,
> through ceaseless struggles and confrontations, transforms,
> strengthens, or reverses them; as the support which these force rela-
> tions find in one another, thus forming a chain or a system, or on
> the contrary, the disjunctions and contradictions which isolate them
> form one another; and lastly, as the strategies in which they take
> effect, whose general design or institutional crystallization is
> embodied in the state apparatus, in the formulation of the law, in
> the various social hegemonies. . . . Power is everywhere; not because
> it embraces everything, but because it comes from everywhere.[34]

Despite Foucault's concern throughout his work with the effect of power on the body, such a passage describes power as being almost entirely disembodied. Power is "embodied in the state apparatus, in the formulation of law, in . . . social hegemonies," not in any one particular body. Power is not something which "embraces"—as a body might; rather it comes from everywhere. It is multivalent and elusive. Traditional scholarship has, of course, devoted much effort to elucidating the trope of the body politic, especially as it relates to the concept of monarchy, and this work is fundamental for any-one trying to understand the concept.[35] But, as texts like *La cazzaria* make clear, the body politic is not just an ideal body, it is also a gendered body and—as we shall see—a sexual body.

In its awareness of the realities of power and its pessimism about peaceful resolution of civic conflict, Vignali's political vision is strikingly similar to that of Machiavelli, whose theories were shaped by the same period of Italian political disunity and communal strife. *La cazzaria* never mentions Machiavelli directly, but it is not hard to sense his influence. Arsiccio's observation that "all the most learned men of our time study nothing else but tyrannical power" (125–26) is followed immediately by a parodic reference to Livy, the Roman historian who was the subject of Machiavelli's *Discourses*.

Like Vignali, Machiavelli also conceived of the body politic as both gendered and sexualized. As John Freccero has pointed out, for Machiavelli the body politic is always female: "the state or realm is like a spouse to the ruler who possesses her."[36] Freccero points first to Machiavelli's famous statement in *The Prince* that "Fortune is a lady and the man who holds her down must beat and bully her"[37] and then to the passage in the *Discourses* where Machiavelli recounts the story of Caterina of Forlì: When Caterina's husband, Count Girolamo of Forlì, was deposed and killed by conspirators, Caterina convinced the murderers that she should go to the town's citadel, which refused to surrender, in order to persuade the citadel's governor to lay down his arms and accept the new order. To ensure that Caterina would not betray them, the conspirators held Caterina's young children hostage. Once safely within the walls of the citadel, however, Caterina appeared on the battlements and turned on the men who had killed her husband:

> she reproached them with vengeance in every shape and form.
> And to convince them she did not mind about her children she

exposed her genital members [membra genitali] and said she was
still capable of bearing more. The conspirators, dumbfounded,
realized their mistake too late, and paid the penalty for their lack
of prudence by suffering perpetual banishment.[38]

In these two instances, the femaleness of the body politic sig-
nifies widely varying, even contradictory aspects of the nature of
a polity. In the former instance, Machiavelli imagines the state (or
the fortune one would need to rule it) as a cultured noblewoman,
who will submit to the rule of a lowborn usurper only if he uses
force; here the female gender of the body politic demonstrates its
vulnerability to seizure by rough and unlawful hands. In the second case, Caterina's display of her genitals is emblematic of the
persistence of the state over time—if one generation is slaugh-
tered or subjected to tyranny, another will rise to claim its lawful
rights. Male citizens are generated by the state as man is born of
woman. Here the female body of the state represents its abiding
and unfathomable strength—a capacity for generation and regen-
eration which no man can completely control.

In both these examples from Machiavelli, the body politic is
imagined as female because of its relationship both to the men
who seek to rule it and to the exclusively male citizens who inhabit
and constitute it. But in *La cazzaria* the body politic is not simply
a female body which must be mastered by a male head. It is a fragmented body in which the dominant gender is uncertain, and there
is no power outside or beyond or above the body which can bring
it to order.

In Shakespeare's version of Menenius's fable of the belly, the
rebellious common citizens are referred to as "fragments"
(*Coriolanus* I.1.223). For what unity can there be to a body which

has a belly, but no head—a body driven by simple animal hunger and not by rational principle? So too, *La cazzaria* is a dialogue of fragments: many social organs are given voice, but the head is not one of them. In Arsiccio's fable the body politic is neither male nor female, but hermaphroditic, having both male and female genitalia.

In Plato's *Symposium* (189c–193d) the comic dramatist Aristophanes tells a story in which human beings were originally monstrous hermaphrodites, having two heads, four arms, four legs, and two sets of genitals. Jealous of the power of these creatures, the gods split them in half, so that they would be forever incomplete. Thus, with one head, two arms, two legs, and one set of genitals, human beings now roam about lonely and sad, seeking the other half that they lost. When they find it, they are filled with desire to unite physically with it and recover their lost sense of wholeness. Aristophanes' comic fable suggests that, although they may appear whole, all human bodies are fragmented and torn. But in his optimistic view, this sense of loss and alienation leads to sexual ecstasy and joy in the union of lovers. In Arsiccio's fable, on the other hand, the fragmented hermaphroditic body is in a state of constant warfare. Rather than blissfully enjoying sexual union, in *La cazzaria* body parts try to screw each other over.

Sex in *La cazzaria* is much more a matter of power than pleasure. Where Menenius's fable sees the body in terms of hunger, consumption, and distribution, the fable that Arsiccio tells Sodo sees it in terms of sexual desire and the power that goes with the ability to penetrate. Cocks rule because they can effectively impose their desires on others. Cunts and Assholes can only hope to protect themselves from violation. Balls are just along for the ride. The body politic remains fragmented and conflicted.

Each of the body parts in Arsiccio's fable represents a different political faction (or *monte*) in the city. The Cazzi, or Cocks, represent the powerful Monte dei Nove, of which Vignali himself was a member. Their characterization as phallic and dominant points to their central role in the patriarchal politics of the city. The division between the powerful Cazzi Grossi (Big Cocks) and impotent Cazzi Piccoli (Little Cocks) represents the split in the Nove between those close to the Petrucci family, and those denied access to power.

The oldest of the *monti*, the Gentiluomini are represented by the Coglioni (Balls or testicles), fitting in that of all the *monti*, the Gentiluomini had the most prestigious breeding, and also in that, unlike the members of other *monti*, the families of the Gentiluomini tended to live altogether in the same house—this living arrangement offering an odd parallel to the testicles' confinement in sacks following the rebellion. And just as the Coglioni are made dependent on the Cazzi and others in the fable, so in Sienese politics, the time of the dominance of the Gentiluomini had long passed, and they were indeed dependent on newer families, principally those of the Monte dei Nove. That Sodo, as a member of the Piccolomini family, belonged historically to the Gentiluomini,[39] adds ironic force to his inquiry concerning the reasons why the Coglioni/Gentiluomini are excluded from the sites of pleasure and power.

The Culi (Assholes) represent the Monte del Popolo, and the Potte (Cunts), the Riformatori, both groups less powerful and of more recent vintage than the Nove or Gentiluomini, and thus subservient in both the political and erotic hierarchies of power and authority.[40] Thus, although Arsiccio's fable mocks the phallic power of the Cazzi Grossi, it nonetheless provides a powerful example of the linkage between gender and social hierarchies in the early modern period. Power is fundamentally masculine, and groups considered socially inferior are represented as being effeminate; they exist to be penetrated rather than to penetrate. Masculinity brings privileges even in defeat. When the Big Cocks punish the other groups for rebelling against them, the Cunts and Assholes are raped and assaulted. The only punishment suffered by the Little Cocks is that they are deprived of their right to sexually dominate the other groups.

It is a paradox of early modern culture that while effeminacy is a sign of weakness and subordination, it is nonetheless often associated with the socially elite world of the courtier. It is the way in which individual members of the male governing class demonstrate their unfitness to rule or their subordination to other men. Thus the male members of the ruling elite who belong to weak *monti* are effeminized and represented as orifices to be penetrated. Those who are truly subordinate—the Sienese who belonged to no *monte*—are left out of the story altogether. Arsiccio's fable is so parodic and ironic that it is anything but a clear guide to Vignali's own political philosophy. However, his sympathy with the Cazzi Piccoli is apparent throughout the fable, and it seems likely he would agree with Cazzetello's rejection of monarchy and democracy is favor of government by an elite group.

While its broad outlines are clear enough, the specific details of the allegory are harder to pin down. Pasquale Stoppelli, the editor of the authoritative Italian scholarly text of *La cazzaria*, has argued that Cazzone, the big prick, represents the hated Fabio Petrucci. Much in the dialogue supports this reading: for example, the revolt against Cazzone is said to occur in Autumn "at the time when the apples ripen" (134), and Fabio was driven from power in September 1524. And yet Fabio was a weak young man whose grasp on power was never very strong and who fled at the first sign of revolt. It may be that a better model for Cazzone is Fabio's successor, Alessandro Bichi, who—like Cazzone in the fable—was assassinated by disgruntled rivals.

Arsiccio's representation of various *monti* by bodily organs is appropriate in several ways: First, each group theoretically ought to play a specific role in the body politic as each organ has a specific bodily function; and just as the *monti* no longer represent specific, homogenous social groups, so too the various body parts no longer act as parts of a coherent whole. Second, membership in a particular *monte* is determined entirely by birth, not by choice, nor as the result of changeable social factors such as profession or income. Just as (in sixteenth-century Siena, at least) one cannot change the sex one is born with, so too one cannot change one's affiliation with a particular *monte*. A "Cock" is born a "Cock," a "Cunt" a "Cunt." That everyone is born with an Asshole is, of course, one of the many points at which Vignali's fanciful analogies break down, but the principle remains that one can no more change one's *monte* than one's body.

HOMOEROTICISM IN *LA CAZZARIA*

An erotic myth that sees testicles as fundamentally excluded from social intercourse is clearly one that puts little emphasis on procreation as a justification for erotic activity. As well as being a political allegory and an erotic myth, *La cazzaria* is also an apologia for sodomy. In this, Vignali's dialogue represents a vernacular continuation of the humanist Latin tradition of learned—and often homoerotic—bawdry.[41]

When Vignali wrote *La cazzaria* Italy had long been notorious throughout western Europe as a hotbed of sodomy. The term "sodomy" was by no means a precise one in the period; it was used to refer to a wide variety of transgressive and nonprocreative sexual activities. In general though, it referred to sexual activity between men, especially anal sex. So strong was the popular association of Italy with sodomy that in early modern Germany, the word for "sodomite" was Florenzer.[42] There is as yet no detailed study of male homoeroticism in sixteenth-century Siena, but Michael Rocke's work on late-fifteenth-century Florence makes it clear that sex between men was an integral part of urban life in Renaissance Tuscany. While homoerotic relations were by no means simply tolerated, and the penalties for those convicted of sodomy could be very harsh indeed, sexual activity between males seems to have been common at all social levels.

In *Lives of the Artists*, Vasari records a story that may provide some insight into Sienese homoeroticism in the early sixteenth century.[43] In 1515 a horse owned by the Sienese painter Giovanbatista Bazzi won the palio, the town's horse race. After the race it was the custom to shout the victor's name in the streets of the city. On this occasion, instead of yelling "Bazzi!" the assembled crowds shouted "Sodoma! Sodoma!"—the nickname Bazzi had acquired through his open sexual interest in boys. The shouting of this provocative name brought the more conservative elements of the city into the streets in protest, and a riot ensued.

This story suggests the ambivalent place of homoeroticism in Renaissance Italian culture. Bazzi's sexual preferences were known well enough for him to have a provocative nickname—one by which he is primarily known to this day. (In art history texts and exhibition catalogues Bazzi is always referred to as Il Sodoma.) He was not prosecuted or punished for these preferences. But neither were they openly accepted. In many parts of Italy the nominal penalty for sodomy was death, and executions were not uncommon, though many cases ended in lesser penalties.[44] Rocke estimates that in late-fifteenth-century Florence "the majority of local males at least once during their lifetimes were officially incriminated for engaging in homosexual relations."[45] But despite the ubiquity of homosexual activity, sodomy was by no means officially tolerated, and in periods of unrest or crisis, preachers like Bernardino of Siena and Savonarola often blamed sodomites for the troubles facing the community.

As the treatment of sodomites in Canto 15 of Dante's *Inferno* makes clear, in late medieval theology sodomy was seen primarily as a sin of violence against God. By seeking sexual satisfaction with other men, a sodomite was going against God's first commandment to be fruitful and multiply. Because sodomites make their naturally fertile bodies infertile, Dante places them next to the usurers, who by lending money at interest made infertile metal breed. There are few activities more dissimilar to the modern mind than buggery and banking, but for Dante and other medieval theologians, the two sins were related in their perversion of God's gift of fertility.

Arsiccio will have none of this; he sees such clerical denunciations of sodomy as obvious hypocrisy and argues that monks call buggery a sin so that no one but they will have the pleasure. Here as elsewhere his logic is resolutely secular and materialist. He goes on to attack the logic behind the Church's condemnation of sodomy, arguing that by rejecting marriage for the "celibate" world of the religious orders, monks, priests, and friars themselves are guilty of the same "unnatural" denial of human fertility that in their view makes sodomy sinful:

> They want us to give up buggery, so that it may belong entirely to them, and make us take up again the cunts they have rejected and disdained. And they go on arguing that it is better to fuck your mother, your sisters, your nieces, and daughters—and fuck them in the most vicious way possible—as long as it is a cunt you are fucking and you are not buggering anyone. And they justify this by saying it is because when you fuck someone up the ass you waste human seed, and thus human generation may be diminished, in contradiction of the commandment, "Be fruitful and multiply." Stupid cows! They can't see that they themselves contradict it completely. Their ignorance and their love of buggery is so great that they do not see that, if this is evil, in choosing to be friars and fleeing the inconvenience of wives and the annoyance of children, they have chosen the way and the method to end and annul the human race, refusing the harsh bonds of marriage and the other things by which the number of human beings is increased and multiplied. (89)

In his insistence on seeing clerical traditions from a purely secular standpoint, Arsiccio anticipates much subsequent criticism of clerical celibacy.

Some scholars have related the high incidence of male homosexuality in the Renaissance to the fact that young men often delayed marriage until they were financially secure. In Italian cities, it was not uncommon for men to remain unmarried into their early thirties. In a society where the only fully acceptable sexual relationship was heterosexual marriage, this meant that many men would have between ten and fifteen years of sexual maturity in which licit activity was not an option. Given the tight social controls on respectable women, this meant most men sought sexual relations either with prostitutes or with other men.

Homosexual relations between men in Renaissance Italy were almost always between adult men and adolescent boys. The adult partner traditionally took the dominant role in the relationships, both socially and physically. As evidence from legal records demonstrates, often the younger men were penetrated anally by the older men, and not vice versa. Generally speaking, the passive position was seen as more shameful—males who allowed themselves to be sexually penetrated were perceived to be acting as women and therefore debasing themselves. Such a passive role was especially shameful in the case of an adult man. Boys, not fully mature, might be allowed to act in feminine ways—after all, their hairless bodies were frequently praised for being smooth and soft, like women's. But an adult man had no excuse: taking the "female" role in intercourse was a betrayal of his masculine identity and the social authority that went with it. As we have seen, this principle is demonstrated in *La cazzaria*'s portrayal of the weak *monti* as Cunts and Assholes, which, in the dialogue's vicious sexual economy, exist only to provide pleasure for the dominant Cocks. *La cazzaria* also provides a more concrete example of a shamefully passive older partner in the story of Brother Paolino, "a friar about forty-two years old," who is severely injured when he is buggered by Brother Angelo, who could not find any younger men to have sex with

(87–88). In most cities, convicted passive partners were treated more harshly than active ones. In Venice, however, the legal penalties were harsher for the active partner, as he was perceived as being the aggressor, and guilty of misusing his masculine prerogatives.

The hierarchical form of homosexual relationship characteristic of the period has often been seen as following a humanist student/teacher model. A pervasive cultural linkage between humanist pedagogy and educational pederasty has been traced by Leonard Barkan, Alan Stewart, and others.[46] Barkan argues that the involvement of humanism in civic politics is marked from the beginning by the metaphor of pederasty—the "first rhetorician of government," Dante's mentor Brunetto Latini appears in the *Inferno* as a sodomite (15.30–33). On a more general level, the Socratic relation between teacher and student carried with it in the Renaissance the same connotations of the corruption of youth that it did in ancient Athens.[47] Possibly "the first proper usage of the term *umanista* in the Italian language" comes in a letter from Ludovico Ariosto to Pietro Bembo, which claims that most humanists are sodomites, and jokingly advises that if one sleeps next to a poet "e gran periglio / a vogierli la schiena" (it is a great peril to turn one's back to him).[48]

Although humanism and sodomy were often linked in the popular imagination, hierarchical homosexual relations between men were found at all social levels, and were, in fact, broadly characteristic of Mediterranean culture over a period of several thousand years. Nonetheless, in *La cazzaria*, sex between men is understood and praised as an elite practice, ideally suited to the academic environment that generated the dialogue.

In *La cazzaria*, the elitism of sodomitical sex comes in part from its rejection of the female. Throughout the dialogue female bodies are represented as physically and socially inferior to male ones, and sex with women is seen as a poor alternative to sex between men. While the penis is praised as "the most perfect and necessary of all created things," female genitalia are valuable because they are "the cause of . . . so many pleasures for men" (84). And despite Arsiccio's lavish—and ironic—praise of the female genitals as being liberal, generous, vast, and benign, he makes it clear on several occasions that Assholes are to be considered superior to Cunts. Female genitals are said to smell of shit (a failing the anus is oddly never charged with in the text) and Arsiccio repeats the traditional notion that menstrual blood is toxic: "this blood is so noxious to everything and greatly harms anything that it touches, because it still retains the nature of the original poison" (136).

The anus, on the other hand, is highly praised: "the asshole is the most honored among all the necessary things of life" (94). While some of this praise is clearly ironic, the dialogue is nonetheless quite serious in its celebration of anal sex. Arsiccio is certainly open about his own preferences: He contends that the asshole is the most precious part of the body, and declares that "ambrosia and nectar are nothing but the sweet tongue of a beautiful young man and the profound secret pleasure that is to be found in his soft delicate asshole" (93).

Arsiccio's dialogue is always about power as well as pleasure, and the text's celebration of sodomy is closely related to the erotic hierarchies and power struggles which mark Arsiccio's fable of the body politic. *La cazzaria* attempts to inscribe sodomy as a discourse of mastery in a Republic of Assholes and Cunts ruled by an oligarchy of Cocks. In Arsiccio's fable, being powerful is equated not just with having a penis, but with *being* a penis. The power of the Cocks comes from their ability to exploit others for their own pleasure. Nino Borsellino's contention that "the phallocracy of *La cazzaria* is not a destructive power, but rather a principle of energy that aims to regulate the relationship of public and private forces" ignores the extent to which phallic power in the dialogue is always aimed at imposing its pleasure on others, often by inflicting pain.[49] From the torn asshole of Brother Paolino, to the "wounds" inflicted on the rebellious Cunts, phallic pleasure in *La cazzaria* is marked with a trail of blood.

But for Arsiccio, power is not merely sexual; it is intellectual. In *La cazzaria* knowledge, power, and sexual pleasure are all equated. Eroticism is understood ultimately as *scienza*, what Arsiccio calls "the science of fucking" and the "secret acts of sodomy" (82, 114). This mysterious and hidden knowledge of the natural world is a precious commodity, and Arsiccio believes that—like Latin—it should be available only to a sophisticated elite. But such knowledge is always practical, not abstract. After all, the primary motive for Arsiccio's eloquent exposition of erotic philosophy, science, and mythology, is the seduction of the passive, younger (and suggestively named) Sodo.

La cazzaria records Sodo's initiation into this elite, an initiation which—as is hinted at several points—will culminate in his being buggered by his mentor. Sodo is not entirely naive about his role. Although he may initially be disdainful of sexual knowledge and woefully ignorant of the philosophy of the body, he is not an inexperienced pupil. Of the monk who tutored him, Sodo says, "I know he is learned in the asshole. He studied mine so much that

I'm sure he knows all about it that there is to know" (92). The dialogue begins with both interlocutors in an undescribed location, then moves to Arsiccio's room. At the midpoint of the dialogue the two begin to drink wine, and the text ends with both in bed, with Arsiccio saying they ought to stop talking and let the Cocks, Cunts, and Assholes alone, because they may well do some "good thing" on their own which will give ample matter for discussion the following night.

The dialogue's reader, of course, is initiated along with Sodo. In the framing fiction which introduces the dialogue, Il Bizarro, another member of the Intronati, finds the text of *La cazzaria* in Vignali's study. The framing fiction positions the dialogue as a shared secret, which will be passed around clandestinely from one member of the Academy to another. Only by keeping the text secret will they be able to read and learn more. "Above all," Il Bizarro stipulates, "be sure that no one else sees it but you, because, if Arsiccio knew of this or heard about it, . . . he would be so angry that he would . . . never again permit me to enter his study. . . . But if he doesn't notice this one is missing, I hope to send you more of the same in a similar way" (74). This promise is, of course, addressed as much to the reader of the text as to the Archintronato.

That much of the "knowledge" provided by Arsiccio is entirely fanciful and quite ridiculous does not diminish the seductive power of the text and the knowledge it offers. By making genital organs speak in a fable which is itself part of a discourse of seduction, *La cazzaria* points ultimately at the eroticism of discourse, particularly the elite, humanist discourse that promises to reveal hidden truths and to make the natural world speak. When

Cocks, Cunts, and Assholes speak, they give a lesson in humanist civics. Sexual pleasure is conflated with textual pleasure, and there are hints that textual pleasure, identified as it is with the elite all-male sodomitical world of the Academy, may well be superior. Il Bizarro is able to get his hands on the text only because Vignali goes out to bring him a servant girl to have sex with. It is typical both of *La cazzaria*'s elitism and its celebration of textual pleasure that after having had the serving woman, Il Bizarro admits that he much prefers the book.

The open homoeroticism of *La cazzaria* was provocatively dangerous even in the 1520s, in the years before the Sack of Rome and the collapse of Sienese political independence. As the century progressed such discourse became all but impossible. The rise of a vigorous Counter-Reformation Church and the control of Italian politics by the militantly Catholic Hapsburgs resulted in much tighter controls both on literature and on behavior. The cultural change within the Academy of the Intronati itself can be seen by comparing *La cazzaria* with Alessandro Piccolomini's dialogue *La Raffaella* (1539). After Vignali's departure from Siena, Alessandro Piccolomini (not to be confused with his kinsman Marcantonio Piccolomini, *La cazzaria*'s Sodo) emerged as the Intronati's leading author. *La Raffaella* is his most sexually outrageous text, and it was sharply criticized on publication. Like *La cazzaria* it is a dialogue between a young innocent and an older, more experienced person, and the older person gives the younger instruction on sexual matters. In *La Raffaella*, however, the speakers are both female, and the advice given by the elderly Raffaella to the youthful Margarita is all concerned with how Margarita can make herself more attractive to men and have successful affairs. The dialogue is a conduct book for adultery, and its frank encouragement of extramarital sex for young women led to its condemnation. But compared to *La cazzaria*, or to Aretino's *Dialogues* for that matter, it is an extremely mild text. There is no description of sexual activity whatsoever, and long sections of the dialogue dwell on such matters as the best recipes for facial ointments. Perhaps more importantly, the illicit sexual activity the dialogue advocates is much less subversive than either the sodomy of *La cazzaria* or the predatory prostitution of Aretino's *Dialogues*. Even the adultery advocated by Piccolomini is not promiscuity, but the utter devotion of a young lady to a man who is not her husband. It is in many ways an idealistic continuation of the old fictions of courtly love. All the same, *La Raffaella* was considered a subversive and even dangerous text, and that such a traditional text was thought of this way provides a useful index of just how shocking *La cazzaria* must have been.

SOURCES OF THE TEXT

The date of composition of *La cazzaria* can be determined with some precision by internal references. The debate on the status of the Italian language draws on Bembo's *Prose della volgar lingua*, which was published in September 1525, so the dialogue was probably completed after that date. The allegory of Sienese politics does not allude to the Sienese victory over the French and Florentine armies at the battle of Camollia on 25 July 1526, nor to the withdrawal of political rights from the Monte dei Nove, which occurred on 26 July 1527. While the victory at Camollia may have been left out as being more an external than an internal matter, it is impossible that Vignali's detailed allegory of the *monti* would have ignored the Nove's loss of civic rights. It is likely, then, that

Vignali wrote the dialogue in late 1525 or early 1526—no later than the summer of 1527, in any case.

Two manuscripts of *La cazzaria* are known to exist: one, substantially complete, dating from the period 1525–1550, the other an incomplete version from the seventeenth century.

The earliest surviving manuscript was discovered in 1992 in Barcarrota, a small town in the Extremadura region of Spain. It was published in 1999 in a two-volume edition comprising a facsimile of the entire manuscript, a transcript of the Italian text, and a facing page Spanish translation.[50] The Barcarrota manuscript is a copy in a mid-sixteenth-century italic hand, complete but for the loss of one sheet—four pages of text. One of the other leaves is damaged, but the manuscript is otherwise in fairly good condition.

The manuscript was discovered in the course of the demolition of an old house, and bound with it was a diverse collection of ten printed books, published for the most part in 1538–1543. It is not clear at what date these texts were bound together. Most of them were published outside Spain and several languages are represented: French, Italian, and Portuguese, as well as Spanish. Their subject matter is similarly varied—including Catholic devotional texts, Huguenot poetry, and the picaresque novel *Lazarillo de Tormes*.

There has been much speculation on who may have owned the volume. The editors of the Barcarrota manuscript contend that this may be Vignali's own copy of the text, but their argument rests only on the facts that the manuscript probably dates from the mid-sixteenth century and that Vignali was in Spain in the early 1540s (though in Seville, not Extremadura). They speculate that a humanist foreigner like Vignali might well have owned the diverse collection of books found at Barcarrota. While it is broadly possible that Vignali had some connection with this manuscript, it is not necessarily likely and the precise date and provenance of the manuscript remain unclear.

The second manuscript, dating from the seventeenth century, is in the Vatican Library, MS Capponiano 140.[51] Pages I–77 are an incomplete text of *La cazzaria;* pages 78–109 contain a "Second Part" of the dialogue, in which Sodo recounts his career as a male prostitute to Arsiccio. Although the "Second Part" is an intriguing text in its own right, it was probably written much later than *La cazzaria* and it is clearly not by Vignali. Judging by vocabulary and spelling, it is not of Tuscan provenance,[52] and while the speakers mention the Treasury of San Marco in Venice (f. 81r), the text makes no reference either to Siena or the Intronati. The "Second Part" is very different in tone from *La cazzaria;* the text is largely a series of explicit descriptions of sexual encounters between men, with none of Vignali's joking lessons, surreal fables, or playful commentary. Although they retain the names Sodo and Arsiccio, the interlocutors bear no resemblance to the characters in Vignali's text. In the "Second Part," rather than being the mocking voice of erotic experience, Arsiccio is merely a passive listener who responds minimally to Sodo's accounts of his sexual escapades. Here Sodo is not a relatively inexperienced pupil, but a promiscuous young man from a good family who has turned to prostitution because he does not get enough money from his parents. What he makes as a prostitute he loses gambling. The text focuses almost obsessively on the income that can be made as a male prostitute, and nothing could be further from the aristocratic and academic milieu of *La cazzaria,* in which money is never an issue.

While clearly not part of Vignali's own text, the "Second Part" is nonetheless an important document in the history of male homosexuality. It describes the habits of male prostitutes in some detail and provides many explicit descriptions of sexual acts between men. It ends with a defense of buggery that lists Plato, Alcibiades, Alexander the Great, and all the Roman emperors as illustrious sodomites, as well as citing Jove's rejection of his wife Juno in favor of the shepherd boy Ganymede (f. I07v–I09v). The text concludes by arguing that buggery is forbidden because it is the prerogative of princes, perhaps an echo of Vignali's notion that priests condemn buggery so that they can keep such pleasures for themselves. These few concluding pages are the only portion of the text that is vaguely reminiscent of the playfully intellectual tone of Vignali's work. They include a brief debate over the etymology of the term "buggerare," and Sodo claims that Cain killed Abel because Abel refused Cain's sexual advances (f. I06v). But unlike in *La cazzaria*, none of these arguments are sustained or developed at any length. Nino Borsellino has argued that "*La cazzaria* is more a philosophical fable than an obscene irresponsible outburst."[53] Clearly the author of the "Second Part" did not see things that way. His continuation of the dialogue ignores philosophy in favor of obscenely explicit sexual description.

Dating the "Second Part" is difficult. Pasquale Stoppelli has suggested that it is a sixteenth-century text,[54] but judging by the handwriting, the manuscript itself was probably written in the seventeeth century, and its existence is not firmly attested until I724, the date it entered the Vatican Collections. There is little internal evidence for dating, though at one point (f. 99v) a character appears armed with a pistol, uncommon before the late sixteenth century.

Perhaps the most interesting passage of the dialogue is its description of oral sex. Like masturbation, oral sex is almost never mentioned in Renaissance texts, and when mentioned it is almost always described with disgust.[55] Besides giving a good indication of the tone of the dialogue, the following passage is interesting in its treatment of oral sex as something odd and frightening, and yet ultimately pleasurable. Sodo meets a sacristan outside a church and goes back with him to his room for sex:

> After much talk he pulled out his enormous thing and I began
> to stroke it while he kissed me, and he caressed mine too. And
> when he saw that my standard was raised, he went down on the
> ground and opening his mouth, took it inside with the greatest
> daring, saying that I should act as if I was getting fucked.
> Consider how great my fear was to see him swallow up my poor
> cock like a hungry wolf, thinking that he wanted to tear it out
> right where it stood. (f. 84v–85r)

While Sodo ends by finding the experience somewhat pleasurable, his overall reaction is one of frightened bewilderment.

The Capponiano copy of Vignali's text lacks the introductory letter as well as the marginal *quaestiones*. Some of the debate over the Italian language is omitted, and the text ends abruptly as the various organs are debating how to punish the traitorous testicles. Minor errors and changes in the text suggest that the Capponiano manuscript is not copied from either of the surviving print editions of *La cazzaria*. It also appears to be independent of the Barcarrota manuscript. Because of its late date, Pasquale Stoppelli, *La cazzaria*'s Italian editor, contends that its textual value is insignificant; the editors of the Barcarrotta manuscript disagree, arguing that it may derive from a source text that predates both surviving print editions. This seems unlikely, but given the paucity of evidence of early manuscripts and print copies of the text, it is impossible to determine how close the Capponiano manuscript is to Vignali's original.

Only two sixteenth-century printed copies of *La cazzaria* are known to survive, both in the Bibliothèque Nationale in Paris (Enfer 565 and 566).[56] They are both different editions, and Enfer 565 (EI) seems to derive from 566 (E). [57] Both Enfer 565 and 566 are octavo volumes of ninety-one pages—small books which could easily be carried or concealed. Though the first six pages of 566 are missing, both texts are identically paginated. They differ, however, in that Enfer 565 prints the marginal topic headings in the external margins, whereas in Enfer 566 they are always in the left margin. Enfer 565 has a manuscript note on Vignali on the title page written by the bibliographer Giuseppe Molini and dated "Paris, 19 Germinal l'an 8"—that is, 8 April 1800. Both texts have minor errors of spelling: Enfer 565 corrects some of those found in 566 and on this basis Stoppelli has judged that 565 derives from 566.

Neither text is dated, though they appear to be from the 1530s. It is uncertain whether either of them is the first edition of the text. Stoppelli argues that the errors in 566 prove it could not be the first printed copy, but given the conditions in which illicit texts were printed in the sixteenth century, it is quite possible that even the first printing could have been rushed and careless, especially if, as seems likely, Vignali had nothing to do with the printing of his text. A copy of another sixteenth-century edition, published in Naples but now lost, was described by the nineteenth-century French bibliographer J. C. Burnet.[58]

The present translation is based on Stoppelli's Italian text, which collates E and EI—the earliest printed sources. The Barcarrota manuscript, which may indeed be the earliest surviving version, differs very little in substance from the printed texts that Stoppelli used—the differences are primarily in the use of alternate Italian morphology and vocabulary whose significant distinctions disappear when translated into English.[59] Despite the claims recently made for the Capponiano manuscript by the editors of the Barcarrota text, it remains an incomplete seventeenth-century copy of uncertain provenance, and thus not useful as a text on which to base a modern English translation.

DISSEMINATION OF THE *LA CAZZARIA* IN THE SIXTEENTH CENTURY AND AFTER

Although surviving copies are rare, *La cazzaria* was clearly circulating in at least two different editions, and probably more, as early as the 1530s. The text had evidently accumulated some notoriety by 1541, when it appears as the subject of one of Niccolò Franco's sonnets in *Priapea:*

> Priapo, io son l'Arsiccio Intronato
> E nell'intronataggine il maggiore,
> Ch'oggi per farti un profumato onore
> Un mio libbretto in dono t'ho recato
>   Qui sono tutti i cazzi d'ogni stato,
> Cazzi da poco, e cazzo di valore,
> Cazzi da donne vedove, e da Suore,
> Cazzi da Granmaestro, e da Prelato,
>   Cazzi da non toccar se non co' guanti
> Cazzi da donna quando si marita,

E cazzi scarsi, e cazzi traboccanti.

E per farsi *La cazzaria* ben fornita
Vi sono i cazzi a millioni, e quanti
Pietro Aretino n'ha provati in vita.

Priapus, I am Arsiccio Intronato, the greatest of the
Stunned. And today to pay you sweet-smelling homage, I have
made you a gift of my little book.

Here are cocks of every estate, cocks of little means, and
cocks of great merit, cocks for widows, and for Sisters, cocks of
Grandmasters and Prelates,

Cocks that should only be touched with gloves, cocks for
new brides, and meager cocks and bursting cocks.

And to ensure my *Cazzaria* is well-equipped, here are millions
of cocks—as many as Pietro Aretino has tasted in his lifetime.[60]

This poem proves Franco had heard of *La cazzaria* and knew that
it was written by Arsiccio Intronato. It does not, however, prove
that he had read it, for his description of the text is not particularly precise.

A deeper aquaintance with *La cazzaria* is reflected in Benedetto
Varchi's *Ercolano*, a dialogue on the Tuscan language written in the
early 1560s and published in 1570. Varchi defends *La cazzaria* to
Count Cesare Ercolano, his imagined interlocutor, who is critical
of the lasciviousness of many vernacular texts. All the same, Varchi
refuses to use *La cazzaria*'s rude name, calling it instead "Arsiccio's
Priapea"—a Latin term referring to collections of poetry—like
Franco's—dedicated to Priapus, the male fertility god:

Cesare: I have seen [Italian] comedies more filthy and disgraceful
than those of Aristophanes. I've seen sonnets that are even more

disgraceful and filthy than that. I've seen some Stanzas that could
be taken as definitions of filthiness and disgracefulness, and
some that would shame a man just to mention their titles. Yet we
might mention the *Meretrice errante*; and Arisccio's *Priapea, quae pars
est?* [what sort of thing is that?][61]

Varchi: You're mixing spears and axes. In the *Priapea*—and I will
call it that, and not its proper name—at least one finds art and
intelligence [*arte e ingengo*], and the same goes for the Stanzas, at
least for those I think you mean. (2.332–33)

This passage demonstrates that some sixteenth-century readers made distinctions between different types of sexually explicit
text, and that to a scholarly reader like Varchi, *La cazzaria* seemed to
have some substantial intellectual content that helped mitigate its
obscenity. Varchi goes on to compare writers like Vignali to
Catullus, who was the greatest of the Latin lyric poets, and yet
wrote obscene and offensive verses. The speakers rehearse the old
argument that writers may deal with lascivious material and still
live chaste lives. But ultimately Varchi is critical of such rhetorical
excuses, and the dialogue goes on to praise poets like Dante and
Petrarch who wrote of love without sexually explicit detail.

Political and social developments in Italy after 1560 ensured
that *La cazzaria* would not receive even the grudging respect Varchi
gives it. The general loss of Italian political independence and the
triumph of the Counter-Reformation Church led to a more
repressive intellectual environment throughout the peninsula.
After Varchi, texts mentioning, and even praising, Antonio Vignali
no longer mention *La cazzaria*. The change in social climate from
the 1520s to the 1570s can best be gauged by comparing *La caz-*

zaria to another dialogue produced by the Intronati—Girolamo Bargagli's *Dialogo de giuochi che nelle vegghie sanesi si usano di fare* (Dialogue on the Games which Used to Be Played in Siena in the Old Days), first published in 1572. In this dialogue, which Nino Borsellino has rightly called an "anti-*Cazzaria*," the discussion deals not with sodomy, sexual power, and republican politics, but rather with flirtatious parlor games played in groups of aristocratic young men and women.

The contrast between the two dialogues is sharpened by the fact that the main speaker in the *Dialogo de giuochi* is none other than Sodo. Rather than being a young, sexually ignorant pupil, in Bargagli's text Sodo is an elderly man, returning to Siena after a long absence as an almost heroic figure. Political turmoil has resulted in the banning of the Intronati, and a group of young Sienese are hoping to rebuild the Academy. They turn to Sodo for advice and counsel, since he was one of the Academy's founding members.

Sodo praises many of the early members of the Academy (sig. B3v), but never mentions Vignali. He tells the young men that two things are necessary for an Intronato to succeed in the world: "one is the protection of those in power, the other is the favor of the most powerful ladies. For these two sources of power are like rain and sun to your genius; without them, even if your wits are fertile, your labors will never bear any significant fruit" (sig. B4r). No doubt this is excellent advice, but nothing could be further from the spirit of *La cazzaria* with its contempt for established authorities in Church and State, and its disdain for women.

Bargagli's dialogue not only advises seeking women's favor, it is in many ways a handbook on how to get it. *Dialogo de giuochi* is dedicated to Isabella de'Medici Orsina, the duchess of Bracciano, and the games it describes are all flirtatious ones in which young men tease young women about love in a group setting. Examples include game 35, "The Temple of Venus" in which young men kneel and beg favors of one of the ladies, who pretend to be the goddess of love, and game 99, "The Hunt for Love" in which young men stage a mock hunt for the "beast of love" which is found in the eyes of one lady or another. The final game, number 130, is actually entitled "How to Gain the Favor of your Beloved." Though there is always a sexual undertone, the games are unfailingly polite, and always played publicly among a large group of well-bred men and women. Such games are presented by Sodo as being the primary activity of the Intronati in their earliest days. Bargagli probably knew better, but the Intronati were indeed banned at the time he wrote his dialogue, and he also knew that if the Academy was to be reestablished, it would have to distance itself from its rebellious and sodomitical past.

Although *La cazzaria* was no longer openly mentioned, copies of it still existed, and it circulated both in manuscript and in print. By the end of the sixteenth-century the dialogue was known—at least by reputation—as far away as England. At least two sixteenth-century Londoners were aware of the volume: John Florio's 1598 Italian-English dictionary, *A Worlde of Words* (STC 11098) provides the first English translation of the dialogue's title: the Italian "Cazzaria" is defined as "a treatise or discourse of pricks." The term "cazzo," for "penis," was actually fairly current in London if its appearance in English plays and poems is any indication: Ben Jonson, in particular, was fond of using it: in *Every Man Out of His Humor* (1599) there is talk of "nimble-spirited Catso's" (2.1.21), and in *Cynthia's Revels* (1600) the dissolute courtier Hedon frequently exclaims "Od's so."

In addition to the reference in Florio's dictionary, John Wolfe's preface to his 1584 London edition of Pietro Aretino's *Ragionamenti* promises the reader that the appearance of that volume will be followed by the publication of similar works, including "il comune de l'Arsiccio" (Arsiccio's comune; sig. A2)—a clear reference to *La cazzaria*. Wolfe was a London printer with extensive Italian connections, and he published works by both Machiavelli and Aretino in London in the 1580s.[62] But his promised edition of *La cazzaria* never appeared.

Sections of *La cazzaria* were later incorporated into the erotic classic *Il libro del perchè* or, as it was known in eighteenth-century England, *The Why and the Wherefore*.[63] One of the earliest items to find its way into the Private Case of the British Library is a copy of *Il libro del perchè* from the collection of George III.[64] The *Libro* appeared as early as 1765, and exists in both Italian and English versions, both published mainly in Paris. The Italian version is a fifty-six-page narrative poem in three parts; the first is a mock epic retelling of the overthrow of Cazzone; the second reworks the story of the women's petition to Jove that men be given bigger genitals. The third is a tale of an ardent lover who at the last minute becomes impotent—a common theme in erotic writing of the late seventeenth and eighteenth centuries, but which has no connection to *La cazzaria*. *Libro del perchè* provides a good example of the progressive trivialization of *La cazzaria*. Detached from their original social and political contexts, the materials of Vignali's dialogue reappear merely as bawdy comic tales.

SUBSEQUENT EDITIONS

The first modern edition of *La cazzaria* was published in Italian in Brussels in 1863. This edition was edited by E. Cléder, and gave its place of publication as Cosmopoli—a false name used in many editions of erotic texts in the sixteenth century, including John Wolfe's London editions of Aretino published in the 1580s. This volume was printed in a limited edition of one hundred copies, and contains the Italian text of the dialogue as well as an eighty-one-page introduction in French, dealing primarily with the history of the Intronati.

The French translation by Alcide Bonneau (Paris: Lisieux, 1882) soon followed. Bonneau's text, part of a series of vintage erotic texts published for collectors by Isidore Lisieux, printed the original Italian text with a facing-page French translation. Again there was a substantial introduction in French.

A German translation, edited by G. Vorberg, appeared in the 1920s, with a postscript by W. Stekel, a Viennese psychoanalyst who worked with Freud (Stuttgart: J. Putnam, 1924). In his post-script, Stekel argues that *La cazzaria* is "a historical-cultural document of the greatest importance." He treats the text not as a literary work, but as documentary evidence of private conversation between men in a period when "sexuality was still seen as the central aspect of life"—a period of imagined frankness which he contrasts with the repressed state of twentieth-century European sexual mores. Stekel marvels at the centrality of homosexuality in the text and argues that, like modern children, Renaissance adults were clearly in a state of anal fixation. *La cazzaria*, he concludes, "presents us with 'eternal humanity,'" and "confirms the old saying that even mud-puddles reflect the sun." Although Stekel's Freudian interpretation of the text now seems somewhat dated, he is quite clear-sighted about *La cazzaria*'s misogyny. He contends that the text displays "a hatred of women almost without parallel"—

a hatred he disturbingly suggests is shared by many of his own neurotic male patients.

A later German edition, entitled *Die Cazzaria* was published in the early 1960s (Hamburg: Gala Verlag, 1963). Another, edited by Giovanni Ravasio and Klaus G. Renner was published in the 1980s (Munich: K. G. Renner, 1988).

The most scholarly rigorous edition of *La cazzaria* is the Italian edition by Pasquale Stoppelli and Nino Borsellino (Rome: Edizioni dell'Elefante, 1984), with an excellent introduction and detailed textual notes. On the other hand, the most recent French edition, edited by Jean-Paul Rocher (Cognac, 1996), has no critical apparatus whatsoever.

In his catalogue of the British Library Private Case, Patrick J. Kearney claims that two different English translations of *La cazzaria* were published in California in 1968: The first, translated by Rudolphe Schleifer, was apparently entitled *The Love Academy* (Brandon House, 1968); the second, credited to "Sir Hotspur Dunderpate," was translated by Samuel Putnam and published as *Dialogue on Diddling: La cazzaria* (City of Industry, Calif.: Collectors Publications, 1968). A copy of this text is in the UCLA library. These editions did not circulate widely, nor if their titles are any indication, were they very accurate translations. Samuel Putnam's 1920s translations of Aretino are extremely inaccurate.

OTHER WORKS BY VIGNALI

It is difficult to ascertain the effect that the writing of *La cazzaria* had on Vignali's career. As we have seen, almost all references to him by later biographers praise both his wit and his skill as a writer. And yet he produced no other major work. The publication of *La cazzaria* must have caused Vignali a good deal of embarrassment, if not worse; the text's dissemination may have had something to do with his decision to leave Siena, and perhaps *La cazzaria*'s unwelcome notoriety explains why he published nothing else in his lifetime. However, a handful of texts by Vignali do survive, both posthumously published and unpublished, and although none have the energy and originality of *La cazzaria*, they nonetheless offer some insight into the subsequent life and tastes of its author.[65]

The biographical sketch of Vignali in Ugurgieri-Azzolini's *Le pompe sanesi* makes no reference to *La cazzaria*, but focuses instead on Vignali's authorship of "that capricious and ingenious letter in which every phrase is a Sienese proverb." This odd text was first published in Siena in 1571, in a volume entitled *Alcune lettere amorose, una dell'Arsiccio Intronato, in proverbi, l'altro di Alessandro Marzi, Cirloso Intronato, con le risposte e con alcune sonetti* (Some Amorous Letters, One by Arsiccio Intronato, in Proverbs, the Other by Alessandro Marzi, Cirloso Intronato, with the Replies and Several Sonnets).[66] As the title indicates, besides Vignali's letter, the volume also includes an exchange of letters and sonnets between Alessandro Marzi (Cirloso Intronato) and a certain Madonna Persia, in which he begs to become her lover and she refuses.

Vignali's letter, while addressed to his Most Noble Lady, is not at all amorous. It is a twelve-page tissue of proverbs, one after the other. It begins with a portentous promise to speak plainly:

> Now that I am safe, as someone said, I want to drop this mask
> and I do not intend to play the hypocrite. My little sister, you
> have fooled yourself to believe that this Arsiccio, who used to
> play the fool, was a good man. He was more false, more wicked,
> and more malicious than the devil in Hell.

But rather than speaking plainly, the text immediately tumbles into a relentless series of proverbs, of which the following excerpt may provide a representative example:

> He who misses one point misses one hundred, and he is not
> entirely wise who does not know when to be a fool, or indeed an
> Intronato. I'd rather lose my finger than my hand, and to have
> the blame but not the ridicule, so that it would not be said that I
> was horned, or beaten, or made to dance, until now I feel a whis-
> tle in my ears and it seems to say to you, this tale-teller Arsiccio
> of yours, I don't understand him, and I do not wish you to speak
> with your mouth wide open, nor to put fleas in other people's
> ears in this way.

Ugurgieri-Azzolini claims that Arsiccio's torrent of proverbs contains hidden political meanings: "he who well considers it knows that in speaking to Love and lamenting the loss of his beloved, he is mourning his homeland under the name of his Lady, and he throws in her face the wrong she has done him, with good political points, but hidden." To a modern reader, however, Vignali's *Letter* is so unspecific that it is difficult to ascertain any political message in it—hidden or otherwise. When he declares that "I will therefore be an Intronato, and speak in proverbs like a crazy man" (8), it is hard not to take him at his word. But it is nonetheless significant that the author of *La cazzaria* was remembered in his city as a man who spoke his political conscience, even under the cover of allegory and wordplay. For whatever reason, the volume containing Vignali's letter was popular enough to be reprinted several times in the years following its first publication. Scipione Bargagli's *Il Turamino* (1602) also praises Vignali for his "most pleasing and witty letter," and claims that "no one was born with better diction in vernacular prose, or had a better style than Arsiccio" (VII.23–25).

Like the *Letter*, Vignali's play *La Floria* was also posthumously published—by Giunti in Florence in 1560, and it must have had some success, for it was reprinted in 1567. In contrast to the baffling and eccentric *Letter*, this comedy, written for the monks of San Bernardino late in Vignali's life, is entirely conventional, though its language and humor are sometimes a bit coarse. In the preface to the play, defending his text from its detractors, Vignali offers a concise summary of the plot:

> In this comedy . . . there is nothing dishonorable. For it deals
> only with Fortunio, a Florentine gentleman in love with Floria,
> the servant of a pimp called Filarco, and he seeks with decep-
> tions to get his hands on her. And following the plan of one of
> his servants, puts him in danger of losing his goods and his life.
> Roberto Fregoso, a Genoese, arrives unexpectedly, and finding
> that the beloved young woman is his daughter, gives her in mar-
> riage to the lovesick Fortunio. Now if you see anything in this
> that could be evil or wicked, or that might be obscene—though
> I don't believe it—let it go and find the good in it. (sig. A2v)

As this summary suggests, *La Floria* is a conventional romantic comedy, and while it seems to have been criticized in some circles for its occasional crude language, it bears little resemblance to *La cazzaria*.

The only similarity between the two texts is Vignali's habitual disgust with the female body, which is briefly evident in an early scene in the play in which Floria and her elderly female companion Elena have the following exchange:

> *Elena*: You know, Floria, it is the same with us as with tuna—if it
> is not well washed, rubbed, cooked, and dressed with vinegar, it
> stinks, is filthy, and is so disgusting that people not only don't
> want to touch it, they don't want to be near anyone who has
> touched it. So too are we women, who without ointments and
> perfumes would not find a dog or a cat who would nuzzle us.
>
> *Floria*: But what part of us smells?
>
> *Elena*: Let it be enough for you that we do; it's bad enough that
> others speak badly of us, without us listing our defects ourselves.
>
> (Act I.2; sig. A6r)

As this passage suggests, Floria is an impossibly naive and idealized character: though she was kidnapped by Filarco the pimp
when she was just a child, she insists that she has remained a virgin (Act 3.5; sig. E3r), and she criticizes other women harshly for
using cosmetics and perfumes:

> Oh, I've seen that all this morning up till now the two of us did
> not rest a minute from washing ourselves, polishing ourselves,
> cleaning ourselves, plucking ourselves, rubbing ourselves, clipping
> ourselves, smoothing ourselves, and squishing ourselves, so much
> that I'd almost say we pissed ourselves. I have rubbed myself so
> thoroughly that I feel utterly worn through.
>
> (Act I.2; sig. A5v)

Although such criticism of female bodies and habits is found in
many similar texts of the period, it nonetheless reprises a prominent theme of *La cazzaria*. It is perhaps significant that the only
female protagonist in Vignali's work is impossibly chaste and very
critical of women as a group. Overall, however, Floria is a passive

and dull character, and she barely appears in the play to which she gives her name.

No other plays were attributed to Vignali in his lifetime or in later years, although in the 1980s Mireille Celse-Blanc argued that Vignali is the probable author of the anonymous play *Aurelia*, which survives only in one manuscript, discovered in South Africa in 1938.[67] Although the play has connections to Siena and seems to be from the sixteenth century, her arguments linking the text with Vignali are all circumstantial and ultimately unconvincing, especially given the Intronati's habit of communal authorship.

In *Il Turamino*, Scipione Bargagli claims that Vignali had written "a few tales and other dialogues of love" (VII.23–25). It is unclear whether by this he means *La cazzaria*. No other prose dialogues by Vignali are known to exist. There are manuscript copies, however, of several poems attributed to him. The most elaborate of these poems is his Italian blank verse translation of Books XI and XII of Virgil's *Aeneid*, dedicated to Camilla Saracini, a copy of which is in the Archivo Storico Civico and Biblioteca Trivulziana in Milan, MS 1110. Another copy, containing only Book XI, is in the Biblioteca Nazionale in Florence, MS Palatino 381.

Besides these translations, three original poems are attributed to Vignali in surviving manuscripts: a blank verse mythological narrative poem called *Antiopea*; a Horatian verse satire, beginning "Quanto più col cervel girando a torno"; and a short obscene lyric, entitled *A la gratia*.[68] *Antiopea* and the verse satire are both preserved in a composite manuscript in the Biblioteca Comunale in Siena, collecting various writing by members of the Intronati, in poetry and in prose. *Antiopea* is a narrative about a Tuscan shepherd called "Arsiccio" whose beloved lady has died. He journeys into the wilderness near the gates of Hell, where the witch Antiopea gives him a vision of the afterlife, in which he sees that his beloved has left the underworld and ascended to Heaven where she dwells in blessedness. The poem is entirely classical in its references—Heaven is as much Olympus as any Christian Heaven, and the underworld is also closer to Hades than to the Christian Hell. The poem seems to be an entirely conventional pastoral, and is interesting primarily because it is the only text of Vignali's that straightforwardly presents his "Arsiccio" (burned) persona as a frustrated "burning" lover.

Vignali's "Satire," found in the same manuscript but in a different hand, is another conventional work. Here Vignali writes of his desire for a quiet life in a little country house, away from the bustle and politics of the city. The poem is Horatian in its praise of a comfortable rural existence and Juvenalian in its contempt for human striving and ambition. Given Vignali's exile (voluntary or not) from Siena, his desire for a place "in the middle of beautiful Tuscany" is more touching than it would otherwise be. And it is altogether fitting that for a heraldic emblem he wants "a burning Salamander"; what better image for Arsiccio Intronato than the legendary fiery lizard?

A la gratia (To Pleasure) is found in one copy in another large composite manuscript of writing by members of the Intronati, this one held in the Biblioteca Nazionale in Florence. Most of the pieces in the volume are love poetry but there are also some which comment on Sienese politics. *A la gratia* is a short, comic amorous poem which, unlike *La Floria, Antiopea*, or the "Satire," mocks the conventions of its genre. Of all Vignali's other writing it is closest in tone and theme to *La cazzaria*, and thus may make a fitting end both to the survey of his works and to this introduction.

Unfortunately the surviving copy of the poem is hard to read—the hand is quite difficult, and the copy is somewhat faded. The main outlines of the text are, however, clearly apparent. After several short stanzas of Petrarchan platitudes about the torments or unrequited love, the poem concludes as follows:

. . . nel dolor amoroso e bel sollazo

Ho mi si rizza il cazo

ond'Amor parla allotta

e dice alla mia donna

questo cazo e nimiche di sua potta

All'hor la donna mia

che pia cermi desia

Del bel sereno cul alza la gonna

e delle rivercie fatto mie don pio

Amor ride ella sguaza a'n col fott'io.

(Palatino MS 256, f. 186r-v)

. . . because of amorous pain and good amusement

I have such a hard cock.

So Love speaks of the struggle

And tells my lady

That this cock is the enemy of her cunt.

And so my lady

Who desires to please me

Lifts her skirt from her serenely beautiful ass

And makes me a charitable offering of her backside.

Love laughs, she thrashes around, and in the ass fuck I.

NOTES

1. Luis Buñuel, *My Last Sigh* (New York: Vintage, 1983), 71–74.

2. The existence of the Private Case was first publicly revealed in Peter Fryer's 1966 book *Private Case—Public Scandal* (London: Secker & Warburg, 1966). The collection was independently catalogued in Patrick J. Kearney, *The Private Case: An Annotated Bibliography of the Private Case Erotica Collection in the British (Museum) Library* (London: Jay Landesman, 1981).

3. Ann Katherine Chiancone Isaacs, "Popolo e *Monti* nella Siena del primo cinquecento." *Rivista Storica Italiana* 82, 1–2 (1970): 32–80, 41.

4. David L. Hicks, "The Sienese State in the Renaissance." In *From the Renaissance to the Counter-Reformation: Essays in Honor of Garrett Mattingly*, edited by Charles H. Carter (New York: Random House, 1965), 75–94.

5. Isaacs, "Popolo e *Monti*," 49–69.

6. On Sienese history in the 1520s see Isaacs, "Popolo e *Monti*," 33–35; Guiseppe Palmieri Nuti, *Storia di Siena dalle orgine al 1559* (Siena: Libreria dell'Opera Metropolitana, 1968) 98–120; and Arnoldo D'Addario, *Il Problema Senese nella storia Italiana della prima metà del cinquecento* (Florence: Felice Le Monnier, 1958), 1–39.

7. On Pandolfo's rule, see Nuti, *Storia*, 99–109.

8. Benvoglienti, Miscellanea, Biblioteca Communale di Siena, MS. C. V. 13, f. 338. The most detailed recent account of Vignali's life appears in Mireille Celse-Blanc's edition of the anonymous play *Aurelia: Aurelia: Edition Critique. Centre Universitaire de Recherche sur la Renaissance Italienne* 9 (1981), 47–51. See also *La cazzaria*, edited by Borsellino and Stoppelli, 29–31; *La cazzaria (La Carajería) Diálogo*. 2 vols. Edited by Guido M. Cappelli, Eliza Ruiz García, and Francisco Rico (Mérida, Spain: Editora Regional de Extremadura, 1999), xlv–xlvii.

9. Quoted in Michele Maylander, *Storie delle accademie d'Italia*, 5 vols. (Bologna: Lincino Capelli, 1926), vol. 3, p. 354

10. Pancirolo, *De Claris Legum Interpretibus*, 362; also quoted in Maylender, *Storie*, vol. 3, p. 358

11. Lolita Petracchi Constantini, *L'Accademia degli Intronati di Siena e una sua commedia* (Siena: Editrice d'Arte "La Diana," 1928), 7–23.

12. Biblioteca Comunale di Siena, MS. Y. I. 17, p. 9. Reprinted in Constantini, *L'Accademia degli Intronati*, 66.

13. Biblioteca Comunale di Siena, MS. V. I. 1, quoted in Maylender, *Storie*, vol. 3, pp. 355–56.

14. Maylender, *Storie*, vol. 3, p. 357.

15. On the Roman Academy, see Ingrid D. Rowland, *The Culture of the High Renaissance: Ancients and Moderns in Sixteenth-Century Rome* (New York: Cambridge University Press, 1998), 10–28.

16. Bracciolini quoted in David O. Frantz, *Festum Voluptatis: A Study of Renaissance Erotica* (Columbus: Ohio State University Press, 1989), 13.

17. Paul F. Grendler, *The Universities of the Italian Renaissance* (Baltimore: Johns Hopkins University Press, 2002), 45–56.

18. The standard reference work on the academic movement in sixteenth-century Italy is Maylender, *Storie delle accademie d'Italia*, though much of its research is now outdated. See also Richard Samuels, "Benedetto Varchi, the *Accademia degli Infiammati*, and the Origins of the Italian Academic Movement." *Renaissance Quarterly* 29 (1976): 599–633.

19. Girolamo Gigli, *Diario sanese* (Siena 1772), 157; Samuels, "Benedetto Varchi," 609–10.

20. Archivo di Stato di Siena, *Deliberazioni di Balìa*, 82, f. 123v. See Celse-Blanc, ed., *Aurelia*, 47.

21. Roberto Cantagalli, *La Guerra di Siena: 1552–1559* (Siena: Accademia degli Intronati, 1962), 98–101.

22. A facsimile of the letter appears in Cappelli and García's edition of the Barcarrota MS of *La cazzaria*, xlii–xliii.

23. I. Ugurgieri Azzolini, *Le pompe sanesi, o'vero relazione delli uomini, e donne illustri di Siena, e suo stato*, Part I (Pistoia: 1649), 575; reprinted in Cappelli and García, xlv–xlvi. The Latin is faulty in several places and the precise meaning is thus somewhat unclear.

24. Celse-Blanc, ed., *Aurelia*, 49.

25. Scipione Bargagli, *Il Turamino, ovvero del parlare e dello sciver sanese* (1602), edited by Luca Serianni (Rome: Salerno, 1976), vol. 7, pp. 23–25; vol. 8, p. 66).

26. On the Intronati and *La cazzaria* see Antonio Vignali, *La cazzaria: Dialogue Priapique de L'Arsiccio Intronato* (Paris: Liseux, 1882), viii–xii. On erotic works produced by the academies, see Frantz, *Festum Voluptatis*, 9–42; and Paula Findlen, "Humanism, Politics, and Pornography in Renaissance Italy." In *The Invention of Pornography: Obscenity and the Origins of Modernity, 1500–1800,* edited by Lynn Hunt (New York: Zone, 1993), 49–108, esp. 86–94.

27. On the role of *quaestiones* in university disputations, see Grendler, *Universities*, 151–52.

28. John M. Riddle, *Contraception and Abortion from the Ancient World to the Renaissance* (Cambridge, Mass.: Harvard University Press, 1992).

29. Michael Rocke, *Forbidden Friendships: Homosexuality and Male Culture in Renaissance Florence* (New York: Oxford University Press, 1996), 134–47.

30. Pietro Aretino, *Aretino's Dialogues*, translated by Raymond Rosenthal (New York: Marsilio, 1994), 283.

31. Titus Livius, *The History of Rome*, edited by Ernest Rhys, translated by Rev. Canon Roberts (New York: J. M. Dent, 1912).

32. Shakespeare, *Coriolanus*, I.I.75–150.

33. *Sir Philip Sidney*, edited by Katherine Duncan-Jones (New York: Oxford University Press, 1989), 228. For other sources of the fable see Geoffrey Bullough, ed., *Narrative and Dramatic Sources of Shakespeare.* Vol. 5: *The Roman Plays* (New York: Columbia University Press, 1964), 496–552.

34. Michel Foucault, *The History of Sexuality.* Vol. I: *An Introduction*, translated by Robert Hurley (New York: Vintage, 1978, 1980), 92–93.

35. Ernst H. Kantorowicz, *The King's Two Bodies: A Study in Medieval Political Theology* (Princeton, N.J.: Princeton University Press, 1957).

36. John Freccero, "Medusa and the Madonna of Forlì: Political Sexuality in Machiavelli." In *Machiavelli and the Discourse of Literature*, edited by Albert Russell Ascoli and Victoria Kahn (Ithaca, N.Y.: Cornell University Press, 1993), 161–78, 162.

37. Niccolò Machiavelli, *The Prince*, translated by Robert M. Adams (New York: Norton, 1977), chapter 25.

38. Niccolò Machiavelli, *The Discourses of Niccolò Machiavelli*, edited and translated by Leslie J. Walker, S.J., 2 vols. (London: Routledge, 1975), book 3, chapter 6.

39. Isaacs, "Popolo e Monti," 56.

40. Ibid., 63.

41. Frantz, *Festum Voluptatis*, 39.

42. Rocke, *Forbidden Friendships*, 3.

43. Giorgio Vasari, "Life of Sodoma" in *Le opere di Giorgio Vasari.* 6 vols. Edited by G. Milanesi (Florence: 1906; reprinted Florence, 1973), vol. 6, p. 389. See also Rocke, *Forbidden Friendships*, 230–31.

44. For Venice, see Guido Ruggiero, *The Boundaries of Eros: Sex Crime and Sexuality in Renaissance Venice* (New York: Oxford University Press, 1985), 109–45.

45. Based on the fact that an average of four hundred people a year were investigated over a forty-year period out of a total population of forty thousand: Rocke, *Forbidden Friendships*, 4–5.

46. Leonard Barkan, *Transuming Passion: Ganymede and the Erotics of Humanism,* (Stanford, Calif.: Stanford University Press, 1991); Alan Stewart, *Close Readers: Humanism and Sodomy in Early Modern England* (Princeton, N.J.: Princeton University Press, 1997).

47. Barkan, *Transuming Passion,* 57–59.

48. Ibid., 67–68.

49. Borsellino and Stoppelli, eds., *La cazzaria,* 27.

50. Antonio Vignali, *La cazzaria (La Carajería) Diálogo.* 2 vols. Edited by Guido M. Cappelli, Eliza Ruiz García, Francisco Rico (Mérida, Spain: Editora Regional de Extremadura, 1999).

51. For a detailed description of this manuscript, see Borsellino's edition of *La cazzaria,* 156–57, and Guiseppe Cozzo, *I Codici Capponiani della Biblioteca Vaticana* (Rome: 1897), 131. On its relations to the Barcarrota MS, see Cappelli et al., xxii–xxiii.

52. Rocke, *Forbidden Friendships,* 284, n. 31.

53. Borsellino and Stoppelli, eds., *La cazzaria,* 23.

54. Ibid., 156; see also Rocke, *Forbidden Friendships,* 93.

55. See, for example, Aretino, *Dialogues,* 284.

56. Enfer 562 is also entitled *La cazzaria,* but it is a poem of eighteen stanzas of eight lines each, unrelated to Vignali's text.

57. See Borsellino and Stoppelli, eds., *La cazzaria,* 153–58, and *La cazzaria,* Lisieux edition, lxxii–lxxvi, on early editions of the text.

58. J. C. Burnet, *Manuel du librairie et de l'amateur des livres,* vol. I (Paris: 1860), col. 1708.

59. Cappelli et al., eds., *La cazzaria (La Carajería),* xix–xxii.

60. Niccolò Franco, *La Priapea,* Sonnet 89, reprinted in Borsellino and Stoppelli, eds., *La cazzaria,* 153.

61. The Latin *quae pars est* is a double entendre: *pars* (part) was often used as a euphemism for "penis."

62. On Wolfe see Harry R. Hoppe, "John Wolfe, Printer and Publisher, 1579–1601." *The Library* 4th series, 14 (1933): 241–87.

63. See Vignali (1882) xi–xii on the relation of *La cazzaria* to *Il libro del perchè.* For editions in the British Library, see Kearney, *Private Case,* items 1020–1026.

64. British Library, P.C.22.C.1; also catalogued 240.C.24.

65. Perhaps the most detailed bibliography of Vignali is the unpublished one by S. Bichi Borghesi in *Bibliografia degli scrittori sanese,* Biblioteca Communale di Siena, MS P. IV. 11., f. 422v–424r. See also Stoppelli's edition of *La cazzaria,* 29–33.

66. Girolamo Pecori, ed., *Alcune lettere amorose, una dell'Arsiccio Intronato, in proverbi, l'altre di Allesandro Marzi, Cirloso Intronato, con le risposte e con alcuni sonetti* (Siena: L. Bonnetti, 1571), reprinted Florence, 1975.

67. Celse-Blanc, *Aurelia*, 28–51.

68. *L'Antiopea* and a "capitolo bernesco" entitled "*Quanto più col cervel girando a torno*" are found in a manuscript entitled *Varie poesie e prose degli Accademici Intronati* (Bibl. Communale di Siena, ms. Misc. H X 5; 2). *Aeneid* XI and XII are in Milan (Arch. Storico Civico e Bibl. Trivulziana ms. 1110) with a dedication to Camilla Saracini, written in Seville in 1540–1541. Another copy of *Aeneid* XI is in cod. Palatino 381 in the Bibl. Naz. Centr. di Firenze. *A la gratia* is in the same collection: cod. Palatino 256 c. 186r.

LA CAZZARIA

*The Book
of the Prick*

1525

IL BIZZARRO TO MOSCONE ARCHINTRONATO[1]:

ALTHOUGH OUR ARSICCIO has always shown himself to be an enemy to women in all his affairs, he is nonetheless as eager for their secrets as a monkey is for crayfish. Now it is true that this rascal only chases after serving wenches—a fact I have marveled at many times. Not being able, myself, to understand the reason for this, I decided this evening to ask him about it. After he had laughed a little at my foolish questions, he gave me a thousand reasons why there is no love in the world like that of a serving maid—and he told me a thousand funny stories about it. In the end, he concluded that filthy, succulent, smutty women are the best fucks—they should be as nasty as possible and if they stink, so much the better. When I laughed at this, he grew angry and asked me if I would like to try it myself. He promised that that very evening he would arrange for me to fuck a certain disgraceful little black girl he knew.[2] After he left me in his study, waiting for him to bring her here to me by way of certain rooftops, I began to strongly regret the delay—as is often the case with those who wait with stiff cocks. So to alleviate my boredom I set about examining certain naughty books, among which I found many sketches of Arsiccio's own composition, and—by God— some pretty good ones. Among the others this present dialogue fell into my hands. Flipping through it and deciding that it seemed nice and short, I began to read it. And thus, by accident, I found myself caught up in the greatest tangle of pricks there ever was. As I read, I began to taste pleasure too great to bear, and I realized that our friend has discovered all the causes and circumstances of fucking. Immediately I thought of you, Archintronato, for you talk to me of nothing else most of the time. Thinking how grateful you would be to see a work like this, and compelled by my many obligations to you, I thought of stealing the book, and hid it close to my breast. Just then, Arsiccio appeared with his slut and had me—to my disgust—fuck her just once, and it made me stink so horribly of onions and stale sweat that for the last fifteen days even the filthiest creatures have fled from me as if I had the plague. Now I send you this dialogue, on the condition that you send it back to me as soon as you have read it. Above all, be sure that no one else sees it but you, because, if Arsiccio knew of this or heard about it, he would be more scornful than an asshole; he would be so angry that he would practically turn into a wild beast, and he would never again permit me to enter his study. This would prevent me from seeing a few other pretty things of his—little trifles that are mentioned in this dialogue, which I have seen and, in part, read. But if he doesn't notice this one is missing, I hope to send you more of the same in a similar way. So read it right away and send it back to me as quickly as you can. I haven't anything else at the moment that I could send to give you pleasure. Remember—if you wish—that I remain your most faithful servant.

La Cazzaria

Arsiccio and **Sodo**,[3] Members of the Academy of the Intronati of Siena.[4]

Arsiccio: I understand perfectly, Sodo, and I'll admit that what you tell me is true. But your excuses are only valid when it comes to speaking with dignified women or men—when it is appropriate to be modest in action and speech. It is different when you are at a gathering of young people, similar to you in age and habits, who get together for pleasure—as was the gathering this evening—where it seems permissible to speak of anything that comes into your mouth.

It may be shameful and disgraceful to start talking of indecent things like fucking and buggery and to fill your mouth with cocks, cunts, assholes, and such, but it still doesn't please me that if such things come up you don't know how to discuss them. According to philosophers, no matter how ugly and vulgar a thing is, it is more vulgar and ugly not to be knowledgeable about it. Your ignorance of these matters seems all the more shameful to me since, besides law, you also profess knowledge of literature in the vernacular and in Latin, as well as philosophy—which is nothing other than the knowledge of natural things. Since the cock and cunt are both natural things, and fucking is the most natural thing in the world and necessary to our existence, it seems to me a great shame that you are ignorant of these things, especially since common, stupid people believe that students ought to know everything—no matter how trivial—whether it applies to their profession or not. I know you've heard the story about the man who didn't want his attorney to represent him in court because he didn't know what phase of the moon it was; from this he judged him to be a man of little knowledge. There was another young scholar of ours who was thought ignorant because he didn't know how to sing at a dance. And because of this inability I know that his lady (who was present) hated him so much that even though she had once loved him greatly and had a great desire to please him, she can no longer stand the sight of him.

Sodo: She must have been with another man besides the scholar, Arsiccio, for it seems to me that most women go around snatching up stupid men, and the more clumsy and brutal the men are, the more it pleases them. I think they hate educated men as much as they can, and I've never found any scholar who was fortunate in love. That's why when I've found myself among women, I've always tried to seem as foolish as possible.

Arsiccio: Certainly it can't have been very hard for you to look like a fool if you believe that. I will prove to you in a thousand ways that in this world when it comes to fucking there is no group more fortunate than scholars, nor any that women are more eager to be seized by. Let's leave aside certain ugly and negligible women—I would rather lose my prick than get mixed up with them—and let's talk of noble women, women of some intelligence. When these women want to get fucked (leaving aside their honor and dignity, which consists only in being able to get fucked secretly), who can they get who will serve them better than a scholar?

Now fucking is a natural thing and every beast and wild animal knows how to do it. When there's a hard cock and both partners are content, it doesn't take much effort to get it. But let's return to the circumstances that apply in the case of a learned woman searching for a partner. She doesn't want the men who fuck her to proclaim the fact in the barbershop or the piazza, nor to have her deeds debated in bakeries and laundries, nor to be slandered and pointed at. Who can she go crazy with? With a vulgar, ignorant laborer? As soon as he's cleaned himself off and laced up his breeches, he feels as if he had just conquered an entire city—it seems like a thousand years to him before he can find some friend or companion to tell the whole story to. So much the better for him if she is a great and noble lady. Most of the time he'll say that she asked him and begged him for it, even that he was paid.

On the other hand, if one considers the wit necessary to find hidden ways and means, one will only look among educated men, who always apply themselves to such activities with an excellent and keen wit. You will find all maliciousness and dirty tricks where scholars are, and you cannot imagine all the sharp and subtle lies they tell about things they want to do. Beyond that, in spirit and certainty of heart they are all—or for the most part—valorous and great. They know what is good and what is bad, which things are disgraceful and which show a generous spirit, and they would be incapable of doing anything that was not virtuous and noble. But most of all they are esteemed for their beautiful conversation, their sweet words, their pleasing entertainments, their jokes and amorous pleasantries, which noble and refined ladies enjoy even more than fucking. In any case, such things are like the delicacy of the food at a banquet—the sumptuous display, the dexterity of the servants, the happy faces of the diners, the spices and sweet-smelling things that make the meal more flavorful and pleasing: they are like the fruits, the flowers, the music, and other things without which, even though the food were laid out in abundance, the meal could not be called a banquet but only a rustic supper.

Ignorant artisans cannot possess such things: once they have finished saying "my love," "my rest," "my hope," "my soul," "my life," "heart of my body," "I wish you well," and other similar stupidities, they have exhausted all their discourse. Indeed, I believe that a poor gentlewoman, who in the face of a thousand dangers has placed herself in the hands of an idiot to get some amorous satisfaction, will be very sorry to find herself next to someone like that after he has finished his brief game of fucking. A scholar, on the other hand, would have a thousand witty sayings, a thousand little tales of love to entertain her, and to make the time between one fuck and the next seem brief and joyful. I'll tell you the truth—if I were a lady I would sooner be fucked a hundred times by a scholar than once by one of those louts. Besides, after the act itself, scholars know a thousand pleasing strokes and sweet caresses which they have read of in books. And because they know what the cunt is like inside, they know how to find all the secret ways of pleasure. I believe that if it were possible for all women to plunge into lust with some student or other, they would never want to see an unlearned man again. But we are few and their lust is beyond measure, and because of this they have to get by however they can.

And this is the only source of the hatred that you think they bear toward us: they would like to be able to enjoy us at their pleasure. Ever since the world began, you will find that only one scholar has been torn to bits by women—the one Boccaccio mentions in his *Decameron*[5]—and that one knew so well how to avenge himself that he has always been a terrifying warning to women against shaming scholars. For scholars have more than a thousand ways of avenging themselves when they have been offended. They have a ready pen and enough spirit to spread malicious rumors and inflame eternal hatred for the person who has injured them. When they receive pleasure, on the other hand, they have a thousand ways of pleasing: with their pens they can raise the fame of the beauty, honor, and virtue of their lady to such a level that praise will redound to them eternally. Thus Dante did for Beatrice and Petrarch for Laura. Such praise always pleases women greatly, and especially those who are a bit conceited.

Most scholars are also masters of enchantments and charms; they know many secrets that allow them to have sex with housemaids and widows without getting them pregnant, and when they become pregnant, to make them miscarry.[6] What's more, they know how to make aqua fortis,[7] cosmetics, perfumes, and a thousand concoctions that would never occur to common people. Common people rarely know more than one trade, and when they share what they know, they either teach it poorly or they want to be well-paid for it. This is not the case with learned men, who always share their knowledge and take pleasure in teaching it as perfectly as possible. Even if scholars had no other goodness or virtue, they are faithful and discreet, and a wise woman, who values her honor above everything else, must seek out such qualities when she goes to get fucked. You yourself confessed that scholars are the most discreet lovers of all when you said you did not remember ever hearing that any scholar had ever been lucky in love. This is because their subtlety teaches them to seem unhappy when they find themselves at the very height of felicity. For all these reasons you can see how foolish you were to imagine that scholars are scorned by women—let alone by women who are noble and cultivated.

Similarly you may learn how many good effects can result from the general knowledge of all things. This labor of ours, with all our learning, is of no profit if it does not please our listeners. To have great wisdom and not be able to show it is worse than not having it at all. There is no joy is having great knowledge in one field if you cannot find men of the same profession to speak with. I believe it is no better to be learned only in law or medicine than it would be to eat only meat or only bread. Clearly it is better to know many things than to be very learned in only one area, for these days you often find yourself among diverse people, who have diverse abilities, and you have to talk now of law, now of love, now of philosophy, now of buggery, now of fucking, now of one thing and another. Because of this, when you are called upon to speak among a group, if you aren't knowledgeable about the things being discussed you are forced to stay on the sidelines or shamefully to confess your ignorance—as you did tonight. Do you want it said tomorrow throughout Siena that at a dinner at Salavo's[8] house when Sodo was asked by a group of noble and gracious young people why the balls never go either into the cunt or the asshole he answered, "I don't know."[9] Oh how glorious that would be for you! Tell the truth: aren't you ashamed of yourself?

Sodo: No. I'm not ashamed of myself, because there is nothing written in my books about such filthy things. My philosophy does not deal with cocks and assholes. And I'm not ashamed to be ignorant of all this, because my fundamental studies have not been in the asshole or the cunt but in more perfect things, which have more glory and honor than these do. Whoever wants to know about these things, let him learn; whoever gets pleasure from them, let him get it. I don't care about them.

Arsiccio: I wish, Sodo, that I did not like you as well as I do, or that I esteemed your honor less than I do: then I might answer you by saying: "If you don't want to know about it, so be it!" And if you wanted to drown yourself, I could push you in and say that you were doing well. But the excessive love I have for you presses me to pull you back from your error and make you see your ignorance clearly and make you put your finger on the fact that the cock is one of the foremost things that you ought to learn about in philosophy. What is the truth when you come down to it, Sodo? Which is the most worthy of all created things? If you want to answer wisely, you will say "man," because you know that both Holy Scripture and profane writers say it is so.[10] Now pay attention. What therefore is the most worthy part of philosophy? It follows necessarily that it must be the part that seeks the most worthy things, and thus it is that which deals with the knowledge of man. It follows from this, therefore, that this "man" cannot exist without a cock, just as it is clear that it is necessary to place the cock so as to close off the cunt and the asshole, and from this it follows that these must be the primary things to be learned. And from the mixing of the cunt, the cock, and the asshole comes the science of fucking and buggery, and thus knowledge itself is enlarged. It is true that these things are not found (as far as I know) in the works of any ancient or modern authority, but nonetheless the cock, the cunt, and the asshole are things that are handled and used every day. It does not seem credible that anyone could be so foolish not to understand this for himself. The same is true for blessed saliva, whose infinite virtues have never been recorded by any writer. But I do not believe that there is any child who does not know all about saliva, or the most part of it, since, being swirled around the mouth all day and then spit by one person into the asshole of another, its virtues demonstrate themselves.

Therefore, it seems to me, since you are accustomed to using your own cock and balls all day long, that you deserved your great shame tonight when you denied that you had any knowledge of them. What the devil have you been doing poking around the asshole if you haven't learned anything about it? What use has it been to you to have fucked and to have been buggered so often if you haven't even contrived to learn at the very least why no one's balls have ever once entered your ass and you've never put yours in anyone from the front or behind?

Oh, the asshole is not so filthy or so fucked that it will not say all sorts of things if you ask it, and not only about this, but about things more subtle and shrewd. But you are such a delicate, fussy little thing that if you hear an asshole speak you screw up your mug as if its breath stank and you don't want to listen to it. I remember that mine wanted to speak of these things many times and you ran away and treated its words as if they were no better than shit. Now you see what such behavior has earned you; if I were you, I would hide myself somewhere because I wouldn't want anyone to look me in the face for a year.

And don't excuse yourself by saying that you want to concentrate on things of greater perfection and glory, because if you mean to say that the cock, the cunt, and the asshole are not perfect and glorious things you'll fall out of the frying pan and into the fire. It will be as if you said that Paradise and heavenly things aren't perfect. For the cock is such a perfect thing that the philosophers have never been able to imagine perfectly what matter it is made of. And from this came the questions of those three girls, who asked whether it was flesh or nerve or bone. Now some people believe that the youngest who (better than the others) main-

Why the Cock Is Called Matter

tained that the cock was made of bone won the prize because she argued that, having it in her hand and shaking it, she often saw it spew out marrow. But nonetheless I find that some others are more believable, for they say that she should be judged the winner not for having known the whole truth, but for having come closer to it than the others, and she explained her reasoning afterward. For perfect knowledge has not yet been encapsulated in any definition. From this it follows that the cock is sometimes called matter or a thing, and for excellence or perfection of matter you will not find anything equal to the cock. In fact it is the most perfect and necessary of all created things since without it neither men nor animals could exist in the world. Besides, I have never seen another animal that can move without bones apart from the cock, which by a marvelous artifice rises to its feet without a bone to sustain it. And besides, it goes beyond all others in pleasantness. Nor am I aware of any other creature so tame in letting itself be handled as the cock is. I am amazed that such a precious thing and such a glorious member as the cock is not always mentioned with the greatest reverence.

Why the Cunt Is Called Nature   But let's let the cock stand there for now and enter into the cunt and consider for a moment her glory and her greatness. And we shall see that the deep and profound things that are within her are unequaled in perfection and sublimity, artifice and nobility. Certainly if we wished to go and enumerate in detail the glories, honors, and triumphs, and the great things that have come from her, all the years of Tithones[11] would not suffice, even if she wasn't the cause of so much beauty and so many pleasures for men. I would sooner count the stars than number her infinite courtesies, her kindness and gentleness, so much so that there is no workman so vile nor scoundrel so rotten that has not been sated infinite times by her liberality. Suffice it to say that she is always ready to demonstrate her great courtesy and magnanimity, always open and spread apart, always accessible, so that there is no fool so vile that he would ever dare to say that she was sparing of herself. Nor to demonstrate her unbounded courtesy does she have any regard for any laws, pacts, or creeds. Nor has she ever been afraid of risky situations; in fact she strives with all her might to follow her inclinations. Since Nature is perfect, she also wants created things, which must observe her laws, to be perfect also. Nature has always been kind, generous, and provident, and the cunt has always emulated her in this, being kind, generous, and provident herself. And so, because of the great similarity between Nature and the cunt, sometimes, when we wish to speak precisely, we call the cunt "nature," as a thing that has perfection and capacity similar to Nature's. Since knowledge of the secrets of nature brings glory, honor, and reputation, it ought to be glorious and praiseworthy to seek out the secrets of the cunt, especially considering the great care wise Nature took in making her to be the mold and habitation of such a noble animal as man.

Sodo: Hold on, Arsiccio! I want to show you that you don't know everything: the cunt is not perfect, in fact it has a great lack or defect, according to what I heard a friar—a good friend of mine—say many times.

Why Monks Invented Confession

Arsiccio: And what did this friar of yours say, Sodo?

Sodo: He said that Nature should have made the cunt with buttons so that you could fasten it or loosen it if a cock is a bit too big or a bit too small, for as it is, it is always too large.

Arsiccio: I would be very surprised if that friar of yours had anything good to say about the cunt or had the wit to say anything clever at all, since all friars are so stupid and clumsy. They are so coarse! They lack the resources to live in the secular world and to support their children, and they have no constancy and fortitude to sustain the weariness and grief of everyday life, so they give themselves up to monkish sloth, covering their vile and bawdy thoughts with shame and with filthy rough clothes, which reflect their morals well enough. And as they are all of one habit, so too they are all alike in malice and fraud; it is not enough that they indulge in all the vicious pleasures that exist in the world, but the pigs want to stick their noses in the cunt, and accuse Nature of not making it the right size for their cocks. Bursting with laziness and sloth, they have nothing to do but plunge their heads into their soup bowls, and imagine ways to fully satisfy their deepest lusts.

This is why they invented confession, so that they could investigate and discover whether there was any pleasure unknown to them that could be found among the laity, and to discover if there were any secrets in the art of fucking that they could use to satisfy their lustful desires more dexterously. But they never had enough energy for me to teach them certain secret touches that I have learned by practical experience in the art of buggery, such as teasing a boy's navel with the tip of the finger to make it push inward, thus widening the asshole, and other similar things. Instead I tell them a thousand lies and, sensing and discovering that they are keen on spells, alchemy, and other stupidities, I appeared so knowledgeable to them that I shamed some of them and led a few of them to break their necks.

I know enough to tell you that when some simple young thing falls into their hands, they press so closely on him that if there is any secret, any sweet or beautiful thing found among us, they quickly gobble it up. I do not want to tell you if they then put it into practice, for it would take a thousand years to prove whether they do or not. But this is true: Brother Angelo dei Servi, discovering in confession that scented ointment was the best thing to use in place of saliva, went into the convent, and not finding any minor brothers, fell upon Brother Paolino, a friar about forty-two years old. They conferred briefly, and then locked themselves in a cell. After Brother Angelo had enough of fucking Brother Paolino's ass with a well-oiled finger, he put a little ointment on the head of his cock, and then he put his proud shaft[12] into Brother Paolino's asshole, which, after it had been oiled, seemed to him like a ring of iron. Brother Angelo, eager to see the entire proof, pushed in without any discretion and ripped Brother Paolino's asshole, tearing a hole more than four fingers wide. Brother Paolino, feeling his asshole torn and sore, began at once to scream. Hearing the noise, several of the friars that were in the church came running, and when they asked what was causing it, poor Brother Paolino cried "Brother Angelo's cock!" The rumor of this spread about so much that even today some are still ashamed of it, and they speak of the cock of Brother Angelo dei Servi, which tore the bell ringer's ass. But don't think that because of this those fools have abstained from following their loutish behavior.

Beyond that, I could quote you a thousand other examples of their desire to experience as many dirty tricks as they possibly can. Take, for example, Brother Marco, of the minor order of the Franciscans, who wanted to prove that putting your finger up your ass while playing with your cock adds great pleasure; and Don Filippo the Carthusian who tied up his balls tightly so that he wouldn't come too quickly: thus his playful fucking lasted longer and his pleasure was prolonged. And Brother Salvatore di Lecchetto, fucking the abbess of Santuccio, tied a cloth tightly around her waist, so that her womb would descend and bump against his cock, and by this brushing he felt as if he had discovered the bottom of the cunt. Don't think that these idiots found out all these things by themselves, since, as I told you, they learned them all from foolish laymen in their confessions.

But let's leave to one side what they do inside the cunt. Worse still, it seems to me, these rogues are devoted to buggery. They have become such gluttons for it that they have adopted and taken over all our techniques. They have become so learned, thanks to their continual study of that art, that laymen are nothing in comparison. And since they have found it sweet and heavenly, and since it does not seem proper to them that any but themselves should have anything to do with matters of divinity, or that other hands than theirs should touch such a precious thing as the asshole, they always forbid poor laymen to do such things both from the pulpit and in those cursed confessions. In the same way, they once hated the cunt, which they had valued so highly and sought so desperately before tasting the sweetness of the asshole, and they forbade that pleasure to us laymen. Now on the contrary they want us to give up buggery, so that it may belong entirely to them, and make us take up again the cunts they have rejected and disdained. And they go on arguing that it is better to fuck your mother, your sisters, your nieces, and daughters—and fuck them in the most vicious way possible—as long as it is a cunt you are fucking and you are not buggering anyone. And they justify this by saying it is because when you fuck someone up the ass you waste human seed, and thus human generation may be diminished, in contradiction of the commandment, "Be fruitful and multiply."[13] Stupid cows! They can't see that they themselves contradict it completely. Their ignorance and their love of buggery is so great that they do not see that, if this is evil, in choosing to be friars and fleeing the inconvenience of wives and the annoyance of children, they have chosen the way and the method to end and annul the human race, refusing the harsh bonds of marriage and the other things by which the number of human beings is increased and multiplied. There is no one who casts aside sperm and wastes it as much as they do, they who corrupt themselves day and night with their own strong arms. They have no room, no bed, no chamber, or latrine that is not full of sperm and thus of unborn embryos.[14] And if our doctrine is true—which I doubt, since I've seen the licentiousness of these friars—on the Day of Judgment you will see so many unfinished spirits and bodies coming out of those bordellos that Paradise will not be able to receive them all.

Besides, if the loss of seed is such an abominable thing, as it is truly according to Holy Scripture, which says that the man who casts his seed upon the ground shall be cursed,[15] and also that the plant which has no fruit (like a buggering friar) shall be thrown into the fire and burned,[16] why do they not prohibit fucking women up the ass? For no other reason than because women's assholes are not assholes, but minor cunts, according to Martial in the eleventh book of his *Epigrams*, where he says that women's pussies and assholes are both cunts.[17] And our own Master Claudio Tolomei[18] in his admirable sestina:

> Love, with sweet glances, and with gentle piping
> Burns the hearts of others . . . [19]

Speaking of women says:

> Their ass is nothing but another cunt
> Nor is it as worthy of honor . . .

etc. etc.

Why Women's Asses Have No Hair

And you see that this is true because a woman's asshole is not honored with the benefit of hair, as is the true asshole of a man, although Musco Intronato[20] with a thousand fables of frogs and mice has tried to give the reasons why women's assholes are hairless. But I believe he is deceived, because the truth is this: their assholes cannot strictly be called assholes, but belong to the cuntish species, and they were given to women so that when they are pregnant sperm will not be cast on top of sperm, thus creating a monster with too many heads or too many legs, as we have sometimes seen happen through the carelessness of those who, when a woman is pregnant, do not know they should go in her asshole, that is, in that smaller cunt. And this is the reason, Sodo, why monstrous creatures are born with more limbs than they ought to have, as I told you a little while ago.

Sodo: That pleases me. But tell me, Arsiccio, if the cunt is hairy, and you believe that women's assholes are cunts, as far as I can tell that suggests that women's assholes ought to be much more hairy than men's, because women have more hair on their pussies than men do on their asses.

Arsiccio: You speak the truth, Sodo, and reason subtly, but I will tell you later on how the cunt has its hair and the asshole its hair. For to tell you this now would be to confuse the order of my discourse, because first I want to respond to that friar of yours, in order to show you how good it is to know about these things. Regarding this, you need to know that the malice of men is stronger than Nature, for it has depraved, ruined, and spoiled all Nature's laws. Nature created a man and a woman, a cock and a cunt, and assigned one of each to each one, and in that time each pussy had a cock to itself.[21] But after war was discovered and the mixing of people occurred, they were separated and divided in such a way that it does not seem that today one can ever find a cunt of the right proportion. If that friar of yours had to earn his bread by studying, as I do, he would have known these things very well, and would not have accused Nature that she had not done well making the cunt, having made it without buttons. I know well that if all rascals indulge in buggery, as I see this one has done, it will not be long before assholes need buttons too, they will be so abused and torn to pieces. No sooner have these traitors seen a cute young man, but they want to take him out of secular life, since they do not believe that laymen deserve anything good, and they would like to deprive us of any good thing or any pleasure that we have. But I would like to know from this friar of yours—if one had to make these buttons, what material would they be made of? If they were made of flesh they would be ripped to shreds; if they were made of bone, or some other hard thing, they would be awkward and annoying to fuck. Therefore, tell him from me, that if he doesn't have more subtle ideas about the asshole than he does about the cunt, then he is a rogue.

Sodo: No, no, I know he is learned in the asshole. He studied mine so much that I'm sure he knows all about it that there is to know.

Arsiccio: Thanks be to God, for you have confessed that what I have told you is true! In short, I pardon him, because the asshole is a very sweet and perfect thing, Sodo my dear, in roundness and capacity similar to the heavens; whence our Master Claudio[22] says:

> O asshole! fortunate above all others
> And similar to the heavens . . .

Nor do I believe that the nectar and ambrosia in Paradise is so sweet as the sweetness that a cock feels in a tender, white young asshole. And if the opinion of Discreto Intronato[23] is correct, that Paradise, Hell, and Purgatory are to be found in this world,[24] and that Paradise is your house, where you live surrounded by servants, master of all your goods, and the angels are beautiful young men, and all the circumstances that make man content are the elements of the angelic hierarchy, and on the other hand prison is Purgatory, poverty is Hell, and worn-out wretches are the devils, then I would like to believe that ambrosia and nectar are nothing but the sweet tongue of a beautiful young man and the profound secret pleasure that is to be found in his soft delicate asshole. And if you want to see and understand what a worthy and perfect thing the asshole is, remember that the Romans, the lords of all the world, having made such a marvelous and stupendous work as their excellent theater, at which—even though a great part is ruined—all who come stare in amazement and affirm that, if all the powers of the world came together to make something similar, it would not be enough, wanting to give it a name equal to its grandeur and nobility the Romans called it "Culiseo," that is, "Culi Seggio"—"the Seat of the Asses"—and that name is said to be fitting for such a great work.

Why the Asshole Is Honored First

Consider next that the asshole is the most honored among all the necessary things of life. For at that time when the parts of the body agreed to gather together[25] they did not want to invite the asshole, since it was a filthy thing, and he, indignant at their great disdain, made them realize that they could not do without him. He quickly shut himself up, not wishing to let anything pass out of the body, with the result that all the food stayed in the middle of the stomach and began to putrefy to the great detriment of all the parts of the body, which, not being able to rely on the benefits of Nature, lay close to death, weak and infirm. It became necessary to negotiate with the asshole, and they told him that he could impose on them any penalty that he saw fit. But since he is so humane and courteous (as Burchiello says in his sonnet "Son diventato in questa malattìa"[26]), rather than kill them or impose any of the other punishments he could have, not wishing to do anything inhumane, lovingly pardoned them all—with this condition: that at meetings he would always be honored first, above all the others. And thus we see even today that at all weddings and ceremonies the ass is always the first to sit down, as befits the leader of all the other parts of the body. Nor may one begin to eat anything, if the ass has not already sat in its proper place. Also, for this reason, most people, when they get up in the morning, the first thing they do is put their ass where their head has lain all night, as a sign that in matters of honor and reverence the head gives way to the ass, because the ass is a worthier and nobler part of the body.

And so we see that, right after the asshole has shit, the eyes want immediately to see the product, as if it were a worthy and marvelous thing.

Why, as Soon as Man Has Shit, He Looks at the Turd

But let's leave all that behind, since I feel it's indecent to fill my mouth with it any longer, and let's return to our discussion of the asshole. If you want to see just how much dignity the asshole has, take care to read the civil law code, the minister of true and perfect justice, which attempts to make each punishment fit the crime. For no other type of assault does it prescribe a greater penalty than for assault on the asshole[27]: it commands that whoever violates an asshole should immediately be burned at the stake, believing that such a person is not worthy of remaining in the world, dead or alive. In the case of fracture to any other part of the body you will see that it must be considered according to the quality and worth of the injured member—and so they consider the asshole to be worth more than any other body part. And for more proof that the asshole is more noble and highly regarded, notice that all the other parts of the body, such as the head, the tongue, the hands, and the feet, bow as a gesture of honor and respect to others—the asshole never does.

And so for a soldier to turn his back (and ass) is such a great dishonor and shame, that one who does so should be hacked into tiny pieces for having offended so noble, so worthy, and so beautiful a thing as the asshole. Not only is it a great shame to turn your ass to someone, but a person who strikes another from behind is greatly censured for it. For that part should be honored out of respect and love for the

Why It Is Dishonorable to Attack from Behind

asshole, which for its gentleness ought to be honored and caressed as a noble and excellent thing.

And you, Sodo, make fun of it! And you are disgusted to learn about a thing as precious as the asshole. Oh you poor fool, how much blame you have brought upon yourself tonight! Oh how much credit have you lost, you petty man, by saying you do not know of these things, which you ought to know as well as the Ave Maria! And if I don't scream at you about it it is because I have too much good will toward you. Besides, I have my own shame to think of, because anyone who knows me to be your close friend, and who sees us together all day, and who hears that, when you were asked about these things, you had no knowledge of them, will immediately assume that I am afflicted by the same error. And I regret deep down in my soul that, in all the time that we have known each other I have not been able to find a convenient time to demonstrate to you how all these things associated with the cock, the asshole, and the cunt work. After all, I am adequately informed about them, and on some occasions they have brought me as much honor as my knowledge of the laws and of paragraphs, so that I can well demonstrate my wit in other things than judging law cases, measuring and surveying fields, discussing the movement of the heavens, curing bodily ailments, leading troops, and other more difficult matters.

Among other things, I remember that once when I was in Pisa at the house of a scholar named Master Giosef,[28] a young nobleman from Lucca, where many scholars of different nations were gathered for dinner, after we had spoken for a time on various subjects, the conversation turned to bug-gery, as always happens when young men and scholars gather. Among other things said on the subject of such mysteries, a certain well-learned Florentine scholar who was there named Il Coia was asked for what reason Nature had put hair around cocks and cunts. He quickly replied that a tap cannot be put in a barrel, however good it may be, if you have not twisted tow[29] around it, by which he meant to suggest that once the cock is in the cunt, Nature provided hair all around in order to insure that the sperm does not pour out. And Il Bellarmato, who was also there—one well learned and prac-ticed in these arts—ingeniously put forth his own opinion, admitting the truth of what Il Coia had said about the bar-rel, but by the same example demonstrating that his theory was false. "Because," he said, "I have never seen anyone wrap tow around the barrel. And following your reasoning, it would be superfluous for Nature to have provided the cunt with hair." And at this point he laughed at the opinion of one of his schoolmasters who through experience had demonstrated to him an infinite number of times, "why," he said, "his cock and my asshole both had hair on them."

Then one Master Hieronimo Ricco, a noble, courteous man from Lucca, attempted to salvage the opinion of the Florentine by saying that Nature had provided hair for both because it often happens that a hairy cock comes into con-tact with a hairless ass, and a hairy ass with a bald cock, in order that, if one part lacked it, the other could supply it. Nevertheless, they were both provided with hair, thus negat-ing the first proposition in the example (that of the barrel and the spigot) because, following that model, the hair would have been placed all around the cock or inside the vulva or the asshole, and this is not the case. It follows therefore that Coia and Ricco's reasoning and examples must·be false. Besides, even if they were true—which they're not—one is not able to say that the hair on the pubes—which is often found to be quite thick—was put there to act as a stopper. And so we have to ask once again why Nature has made the crotch hairy.

Why the Crotch Is Hairy   And so that master subtly considered the question, and replied, saying that if it had not been for the hair that Nature had placed around the pubes, sometimes when men and women are fucking, one or the other of their crotches might have been scraped or broken; therefore wise Nature came up with the remedy of putting a bit of wool between them. And thus those people who package glasses and other things, have learned to place a bit of wool or something similar between them so that they don't break when they rub together. Rough people can put some between their eggs, so that they don't break bashing into each other. "I thank both God and Nature," he said, "for making me with hair around my asshole and making my master with hair around his cock, because he shoves it in so desperately when he fucks me that the cheeks of my ass practically come through here in front, which would be enough to smash up Paradise itself, and certainly if there were no hairs on my ass he would have destroyed it entirely."

He said well, because we are all of such cursed nature that, when we are about to come, whether we're in a cunt or an asshole, we want to get entirely inside. I have since grown in this conviction, and reduced it to a more subtle consideration: that is, Nature having made these hairs, and having placed them abundantly in women's crotches, she made none for their asses because she did not think that women would ever be fucked except lying on their backs. She thought that as soon as a man had discovered that a woman was pregnant, he would want to fuck her from below without turning her over, since it is such a short distance from the cunt to that which we call the asshole. This had the best results: as soon as the man lifted himself up a bit and the woman raised her legs a little they were able to accommodate each other so that his weight was not on her body.

So it is that fucking a woman from the back side—making her lie face downward—is said to be against Nature. Not that Nature doesn't want them to be fucked in the ass at certain times and in certain cases, but she wants this to be done to women from the front: because if, for fear of losing the child, you turn the woman face downward, exposing her asshole, you will be acting contrary to Nature's intention, because the woman will be right on top of her little child, and you will be too, and this may result in a miscarriage.[30]

Why Fucking Women from Behind Is Said to Be Against Nature

Nevertheless, it is necessary to understand these things correctly, for many ignorant people assume that fucking from behind, and fucking up the ass are one and the same. And from this error they fall into a greater one: that is, that buggering is against Nature—a thing beyond all the imagination of Nature. And if Nature had not wanted men to bugger each other, she would not have made it such a pleasant thing.

Besides, she would have made it so the asshole was incapable of taking a cock, just as it is incapable of taking a staff or whatever other thing you like, even though these things are thinner than cocks. Indeed we see the opposite is true, for the asshole can take a cock just as comfortably as a cunt can.

Sodo: Arsiccio, your reasoning fills me with ecstasy. You have enflamed me with fervor and desire; I would rather be cast out of Paradise than to be ignorant of these things, and I want to confess that I'm as shameful as a cock. I feel that I have been entirely ignorant until now. You're completely right, and I know I've done badly not to ask you about all of these things, but I didn't think that fucking went beyond thrusting your cock into a cunt or an asshole until you came. Now from what I've heard, that is the least of pleasures.

Arsiccio: I haven't told you anything, Sodo. But before I go to bed, while I still have the energy for rational discussion, since we have entered into these matters, I would like to tell you— if sleep does not prevent me—about things in this world that, as you admit, you have little understood until now. Since I feel in the mood to talk, let's go to my house and go to bed together. And in that way, in bed, I will tell you some or all the reasons that the balls stay outside the cunt. Those things that I can't tell you tonight we'll save for tomorrow morning.

In order to be brief, since we have more than enough to discuss, I'll leave aside the nativity and baptism of the cock and cunt, and also the reason why they have so many names. I know it would not be unpleasant to you to hear the beautiful debate about putting water on its head or salt in the mouth, which many have thought foolish and many others thought wise;[31] but I will leave this to another time, because I will describe these things at much greater length in a little book I'm writing on the genealogy of the cock—a book I have not been able to finish because of the great disagreements I have found between various authorities concerning its procreation and conception: Pliny believes that it was born of adultery, and Socrates holds that it was not born, but created, and in the *Odyssey* Homer says that Arab merchants brought it from the Fortunate Isles.[32] Aristotle and Strabo both agree in saying that it was born from the slime of the serpent Python,[33] and that it is the poison retained in that slime that causes women's bellies to swell up. A few inches farther on in the tables of the *Autentico*, in the *Digesto vecchio*,[34] it says that it should be a little bit bigger, and reveals the principles that would enable one to reconcile all opinions on the subject. And I found a gloss in the margin of a parchment copy of the *Codex* of Justinian that tells me the meaning of the word "cock" and why the head is called a "bean," why it has a little vein, and why the hole is not oriented the same way the mouth is, but the note is written in Provençal so old that it cannot be understood without great difficulty.

Sodo: Arsiccio, you must not have seen the sonnet that begins "Sixteen women were making a cock,"[35] which deals precisely with why cocks were made and what they do; and everything it says is true.

Why Women Get Pregnant from Fucking

Arsiccio: May the person who wrote it get venereal lesions! I have seen it, and it tells a thousand lies. If women had had to make cocks themselves, there wouldn't be a donkey with a bigger cock than ours.

Sodo: Oh, and do you believe they would be able to take it if we had such big ones? Oh cunts of the world, we would smash right through you!

Arsiccio: Sodo, you just get worse and worse. If you believe that all women couldn't take a cock as big as a donkey's, then you've enlightened me a bit: from what I can tell you must never have read Apuleius, who says that when he was transformed into an ass and tried to fuck a woman he still didn't have a cock big enough.[36] But let Apuleius go, since he might have been making it all up. Don't you know about that woman who came to the archbishop just a few days ago who wanted to annul her marriage because her husband didn't have enough "household furnishings"?[37] Wanting to prove he had as much as any other young man in Montalcino,[38] the husband had to pull it out in the presence of his mother-in-law[39] who, seeing her son-in-law's enormous cock, turned to her daughter and said, "You're feeling sorry for yourself because your husband has a small cock. Oh, if God had granted your father as big a cock as his I would have been the happiest woman in Montalcino. I can tell you that I've seen about a hundred of these in my time, and I've never seen a bigger one than this."

"Say what you want, Mother," the girl replied. "I've seen

our donkey who is only two years old, and he has a cock twice as big. So I thought that my husband, who is twenty, ought to have one at least twice this size as well."

So now, Sodo, you should know well whether or not that woman was eager to take a cock as big as a donkey's. The other was Mona Lisa of San Gemignano,[40] who always felt sorry for herself because her husband had such a small cock. Seeing him on horseback one day, she asked him to tell her where he was going. Her husband knew that the more often he told his wife, "I don't want to tell you," the more she would want to know where he was going. So when he saw that the horse he was about to mount had its cock erect and swinging beneath its body, he thought of a new answer.

He said, "My dear sweet wife, since you want to know where I'm going, I will tell you. My love, you know that I have always tried to think of ways to please you in everything I do. And up to now I don't think you can call yourself dis-content, except in one thing, and in that (by fault of Nature) I have not been able to give you satisfaction—and that is my dick. I have always sorrowed in my heart because I couldn't think of any way of making it up to you. But perhaps my desire to satisfy you and your desire for me to have a big thick cock can both be fulfilled, for I have heard that an excellent doctor and surgeon has come to Colle[41] who has great skill in reattaching members. Our own Lorenzo Gamurini has already been to see him. You know Lorenzo had no nose; well now he's returned with a nose more gallant than the one he had before. He told me that this doctor made it for him from the flesh of an arm. So then I thought

I could have all of this big white cock you see here on our horse attached to my own." His wife, who had been listening to him with great attention, weeping at his tenderness and consideration, felt she already had that cock in her pussy.

She threw herself at her husband. "Oh my dear, don't do such a thing," she said, "it must be dangerous. I wouldn't want to make you do such a crazy thing for any reason. If you came to any harm I'd die of sorrow."

And when her husband replied that he wanted to do it and had his mind made up, seeing his firm resolve, she said, "My love, since I'm putting you in such danger, have him add the black part too. If it's too big we'll find a way to shorten it later."

So if you like, Sodo, you can decide whether she was afraid of being killed by it or whether she longed in her heart to take it. But let those peculiar cases go. You can protest and say that anyone could find one or two exceptions in a thousand. Nevertheless it is necessary that you know that once, in the beautiful month of May, many cunts found themselves in a field where some horny donkeys were grazing. Seeing a donkey take out its enormous tool, they began sadly to lament that Nature, which had placed man above all the other animals, should have given him the biggest member of all, as a great testimony of how much she favored him above all other creatures. But she did just the opposite, since of all animals it is man who, proportionally, has the smallest member. So they decided to send an embassy to the god of Nature to complain of the shortcomings of the male member. For this they elected the hands, whom they had always found to be friendly to them, guiding cocks to them in various ways. The cunts promised many gifts to the hands in return for their pains. The hands, always eager for gain and quick to follow the commands of the cunt, groped their way to Crete,[42] where at that time Jove was to be found. And before Jove they explained that the cunts desired that by the grace of god men might be as well furnished with cocks as the donkeys, horses, and bulls. In order to do more for their part, with crossed arms they prayed that their wish might be granted.

Kindly Jove, who has always accepted the prayers of those who pray humbly, said that he would be more than happy to give them what they desired—if they would submit to the same law that governed donkeys, horses, and other such animals, that is, only to be fucked at one time during the year.[43] "So go back," he said, "and ask if they will want to agree to this pact, and if so, I'll grant what they wish. I would happily agree to grant their wish without this pact, except that I know that would insult the other beasts, and then they would send ambassadors here to ask that I give them the same advantages as women—that is, to fuck any time they want. And if I granted that wish, then men would never get any use out of any of those animals, and besides, the animals would multiply so quickly they would overrun the earth—and not just the good animals, but also the bad and poisonous ones. It would be the ruin of the world. And I, who care for women as much as any other beast, wild or tame, would be forced, if I granted this to them, to grant the same to all the others, since it is my responsibility to maintain equal justice, balancing what has been taken away in one part with what has been added in another. According to these principles, it doesn't seem to me that women should feel they have less than any other beasts—cows, donkeys, horses, or other similar animals—since they can get fucked whenever they want to. This is not permitted to other animals who, though they have bigger cocks, get to use them much less often, and this reduces the advantage of their great size. In any case, if they want to be like the other animals, to show that I want to give them more than they ask for, I'll give men cocks as big as donkeys have. And so you don't have to make any more trips dealing with such trifles, tell them, if they want it, that they will have to go without fucking for a whole week, and then I will quickly grant what they demand of me."

Why Women Always Want to Be Fucked

The hands took this answer back to the women, who were all gathered together in one place waiting for them. They deliberated on the answer Jove had given them, and there was much debate among them. Finally, they concluded that they should under no circumstances accept his offer. And so that no one would get the mistaken idea that they had agreed to set aside any time when they wouldn't be fucked, they spent all that week getting fucked as much as possible. In fact, they figured out ways to get all of them fucked as often as possible—if any of them for some reason was unable to get fucked herself, she invented ways to get other women fucked. And this is the reason that women have such desire to always be fucked.

And so those who, because of their age or other imped-iments are not able to be fucked, are always trying to get their sisters, or their daughters, or their nieces, or their godmoth-ers, or their neighbors, or their girl friends, or their country-women fucked—or anyone else they can incite, encourage, or even accompany to get fucked.

Why Women Help Other Women Get Fucked

Thus it is too that men, having heard of this bargain and dreading having to drag between their legs such a terrible and monstrous scrap—twice the size of an asshole—figure out ways to fuck women as often as possible.

Why Men Try to Fuck as Often as Possible

All this greatly improved the situation as far as the cunts were concerned. However, since they had not been able to obtain their desires, the cunts—as Cirloso Intronato[44] tells us—did not want to honor the promise they had made to reward the hands. And so, the angry hands, in order to take pleasure away from the cunts, grabbed every cock they could find, and rubbed them and shook them so much that they made them come.

And this is where jerking off comes from. Importuno Intronato[45] adds that, to trick the cock, they spit on it. Bathed in saliva, the cock believes he is about to go into an asshole, because you don't have to spit on it to put it in a cunt. Thus believing himself inserted and feeling himself gripped, he comes. So that's how jerking off was discovered.

Why Jerking Off Was Invented

And when the cunts became aware of it, they repented of their ingratitude, and gave the hands very ample privi-leges, to handle and finger whatever they pleased whenever they wanted. And so it is that the hands are always first to touch a breast, to finger a cunt, to slip into a hole, to pinch

Why the Hands Are the First Things Used When Fucking

the buttocks, and to play all the other sexy games, like fingering the asshole while you're fucking, giving spankings, and other crazy things.

All the same, you can understand, Sodo, that if women themselves had made cocks they would be quite different from what they are. For myself, I would not want to be condemned to carry one around as big as they would want, not for all the gold in the world. For Duro Intronato[46] has told me he has seen women who managed to hide a very large squash in their pussies. I once wanted to see this for myself, so I took a large-handled pestle, covered it with ox gut, and then went to see a female weaver I knew. She knew how to do it so well she trapped the whole thing in her cunt and made a display of jerking it off. She said, "Do it, my love! I'm going to come." And, pretending to have finished as well, I pulled on it gently without her even being aware of it. I was completely amazed! It was beyond me, as if I were dreaming! For the pestle was big, and she was a fairly small woman, and I believe she has a smaller pussy than most others. I marveled that she was not injured by my huge handiwork. But she didn't even say a word, as if she had been used to taking cocks of a similar size all her life. Caperchia Intronato[47] wants me to believe that cunts are like water—which has enough room to take a big stone or a small one, if you throw them in. But he never really explained to me the logic behind his analogy. In any case, I prefer the opinion of Soppiatone Intronato[48] that the smaller women are, the more their cunts can take in, because he gave me true and natural reasons for his belief. For little women have smaller legs than big ones, but they want to climb stairs just as quickly. And if they want to build up their legs, they must necessarily enlarge their ass-crack as well, and thus their cunts are bigger than those of bigger women in the same proportion that their legs are shorter.

I marvel greatly that with the enormous openings they have—both large women and small—their guts don't fall out as they walk. And for fear of this women have often decided to make small steps and to walk quietly.

Why Women Take Little Steps

And this is why they stuff themselves with cocks so often; let alone what I've heard about how they often cram themselves with entire shirts and bunches of rags. Some of them even make britches with reinforced crotches so that their guts don't come falling out. Of course they would gladly take a cock, especially if it were fat and enormous, though it would still seem too small to them. And you, you idiot, you want to trust that sonnet and believe that cocks were made by women, an idea that is obviously false, for if it were true, cocks would be as big as bell towers. So you can clearly see it is a lie that women made cocks; indeed, you must know that women would never have been made without cocks.

Why Women Stuff Themselves with Cocks

Sodo: No, I don't know that, Arsiccio. And I will never believe that women were made with cocks if I don't believe it now.

Arsiccio: I didn't say that women *had* cocks, Sodo, as you would have it. I said that if there were no cocks there couldn't be any women. And indeed, it is necessary that before there were women, there were cocks.

Sodo: You're fooling yourself, Arsiccio, because cocks also couldn't exist without cunts, nor cunts without women; from which it follows that women must have existed before cocks.

Arsiccio: Oh that's great Sodo! You've put your finger on it though. You believe that the cock should come after the cunt, and I say that it came before. And if you tell me that the cock could not have existed without the cunt, and I tell you that the cunt could not have existed without the cock: one and the other, and indeed the reasoning is the same in both cases. This question is like the one about which came first, the chicken or the egg, or the hammer and the anvil. Don't believe that this is the first time this question has been raised; on the contrary it is very ancient, and many philosophers and great men have attempted to answer it. Indeed, let's put aside the fairy tale in that sonnet "Sixteen women were making a cock," or that other one "Seven masters were making a cunt,"[49] and other poetic stupidities and trifles.

Why Women Are Disproportioned and Fat Below the Waist

Rejecting the opinion of Plato in the *Symposium*,[50] Pietro Bembo[51] holds that the cock and the cunt were created together in the following manner: When God had created man and woman from clay, to measure whether or not they were the same size, He placed the man on top of the woman, and—being freshly made—they stuck together. Seeing this, the Master wanted to repair them quickly, and without realizing it, in His haste he left the woman upright on her feet, which—because she was still fresh and soft—caused her weight to slide downward. And so it is that most women are fat and disproportioned below the waist, because the matter that made up her widest part slipped and created this disproportion.

But returning to our proposition, I say that when the first Master divided them, all the earth that now is the cock remained stuck to the man's crotch; and as it leaped from the woman, it left behind the hole that today is the cunt—and will still be the cunt tomorrow. And so it is said that women have such a great desire and craving to catch a cock in their pussy, as if they were trying to reintegrate and refill that hole of theirs. And the cock also has a great desire to reenter its proper place. But this story has never pleased me, because, if it were true, it would follow naturally that the pussy would be no bigger than the cock is, if it came from there. Moscone Intronato used to say that when the earth was mixed a stick ended up in it, which had a bit of a bend in it. And so in the pulling it tore a little, as can be seen from the largeness of the cunt. And if he had said he saw it happen, I would have believed him, but he would only say that he *believed* that was how it happened, and so I remained in doubt. Since then I have resolved not to believe it because at that time no sticks had fallen from dead trees.

Subtle Bizarro Intronato, defending Bembo,[52] told me that the inordinately large size of the cunt—so much larger than the cock—came from several things: First, the balls would have been torn out along with the cock, and if they went into the pussy too the hole would not seem so big. Second, he added that when the Master who created us (and I'm much obliged to him for that) saw that the scrap that had come out on the front of the man was about to fall off, he

Why Cunts Take Such Great Pleasure Uniting with Cocks

grabbed it with his hand to hold it on, and while it was initially a piece of earth as long as the depth of the cunt, he
squeezed it together with his hand, reducing it all around.

And from this it is that cocks are made with a bump at
the base of the head; because naturally if you grab a piece of
fresh earth and squeeze it with your hands, you will see that
beyond the area covered by the fingers there will remain ribs
or nodes. And the area beneath the hands came to be
squeezed more tightly than the head of the cock. And from
this it is—they say—that the beginning of the head of the
cock is always a bit bigger than the shaft.

I would be compelled to believe this explanation,
because it is so convincing in itself, since with the subtrac-
tion of the balls and the reduction of the cock my curiosity
would be satisfied well enough as to why the cunt is larger
than the size of the cock. But I have found in certain nasty
books, which must have belonged to the grandfather of my
great-grandfather, a very ancient author who takes up all
these theories. The volume is so old one can barely read it.
He says that if the cunt and cock were created by such a
strange accident then he would like to know which other
creatures were made in this way, under these conditions.
Finally he concludes that all these accounts are fairy tales and
foolishness. Next he demonstrates by experience that the
cock and the cunt were born in different ways, and he lays
out their differing genealogies, and fully lists their properties.
And he takes up the arguments that Dabbudà[53]—an excellent
medical philosopher—makes in his *Paschea*, where he says
that when Nature wanted to make a hole in the man, she

rammed a pole up his ass so far it stuck out in front—and thus the cock and the asshole were created all at once. But he confutes these arguments with a thousand reasons. He also asks a thousand questions about the particularities of the cock: such as, why is it hooded? Why is it not always hard? Why isn't it like a donkey's? Why isn't it like a dog's? Why does it make headcheese? and other most subtle questions. It is true that he speaks confusedly and makes minute distinctions, but I hope, with the help of heaven, to soon bring all his text to light, and to openly speak of its nature with a clear and pleasing style.

Up to now, I've amused myself by paying attention to the cunt, and have taken every care to gain full understanding of it. I have found that it is a great enterprise and each day its substance grows and expands. After having entered into this matter, I want to be sure that I come out again cleanly and honorably, if possible, and then give my attention to the asshole. Having some experience of that subject, I will go to great lengths to demonstrate how much more I can bring to it. I also intend to deal with its sad life and sweet passion, which I have reconstructed from many fragments. It only remains for me to discover what mechanism makes it open and close and pucker up so delicately. The work will be in three books, as follows: *On the Genealogy and Baptism of the Cock*, *On the Nativity and Works of the Cunt*, and *On the Life and Passion of the Asshole*, and I will combine all three into one volume, which I plan to call *Lumen Pudendorum*.[54] Therein I hope to demonstrate just how far my knowledge extends. And in another style, not the vulgar and coarse one I am using here,

I will reveal the secret acts of sodomy, which I have gathered in part from various authors and in part learned from practical experience.

I regret only that I have begun the work in Latin, since, because these matters are universally useful to all men, and affect everyone equally—even those who do not read Latin easily—it ought to be written so that anyone can understand it. All the same, I wrote it the way I did for several reasons.[55] First, to protect the virtue of women, which I have always valued so highly that, if the greatest necessity had not constrained me, I would never have wanted to fuck around with them at all. And thus I've acquired the reputation of a buggerer who prefers boys and follows them around. But God knows I don't think there's a man alive who gets on their backs more often or who persecutes them more than I do. I have a lower opinion of them than anyone else does, and thus they hate me so much that as soon as one of them sees me, he turns his ass to me, as if I were his mortal enemy. So I am hated by one side and the other. But I hope that one day I will enlighten both of them about my works.

The second reason I have written it in Latin is so that certain vulgar, hypocritical idiots who pay more attention to their natural inclinations than to the causes and origin of things will not be able to attack it as a shameful book, when they see words like "cock," "cunt," "asshole," "balls," "assfuck," and other similar terms, which the book is completely full of. This way, when I say "priapum," "mentulam," "nervum" when they read the book those people won't believe it means "cock." Similarly, when they see "vulvam" and "cunnam" written, they won't know these are words for "cunt," and thus they will be happy. That way, though the work deals with cocks, cunts, and assholes, it nevertheless deals with them in a pleasing manner, so that anyone who is able to understand it will take pleasure from it. And thus the delight will be all theirs, and I'll get all the blame and hatred that will come from it.

Sodo: Oh Arsiccio, you could write it in such a way that no one would be able to say anything bad about it.

Arsiccio: God willing! But how?

Sodo: I would write an epistle to go before or after it, in which I would prove that anyone who speaks badly of these things is an idiot. And I would prohibit anyone who wants to criticize it from reading it.

Arsiccio: I would not want to take on that job. Ha! Ha! Ha! You want me to take the bear to Modena, eh?[56]

Sodo: What does that mean, "Take the bear to Modena"? Why?

Arsiccio: What do you mean, "why"? Don't you know how many excellent men have worn themselves out defending themselves in their works against the evil tongues of wicked detractors and all with no success? And indeed their works were perfect, and worthy of the highest praise, and deserved to be valued by elevated and learned wits. Think how likely I will be to be honored since, besides having a coarse style, I deal with ugly and dishonorable things. Nevertheless, I don't want to write any epistles or make any excuses, because I want to allow free judgment and full license for anyone to say whatever they please on this matter. In any case, people will do as they like, and they will never decry it or blame it as much as it deserves to be blamed. And I believe that those who read it only to prick out the bad parts have similarly marked up the Holy Scriptures and other good books in a thousand places. And when they have so many cocks in their hands, they will have matter enough to prick, and especially as far as the cunt and asshole are concerned. But I can tell you well enough that if they wag their tongues against the asshole—if they prick anything in there—it may taste a bit different than mildew. For they—and this is most shameful—have dared to speak badly of its deeds, and it has ways to avenge itself. I myself know well that it will be no use for them to stretch it with enemas or other cures. As for me, I say they can do and say what they like, for I never expected and do not now expect to get any honor or glory from these things. I have written them only to display my knowledge. And if I'm not now able to lay them forth and defend them with the elegant phrases and ornaments which others might have provided by the thousand, it wounds my heart. It is true that I could keep these works to myself and correct them when I have better learned the art of writing and the rules of composition, which I have not mastered yet, but in any case these are uncertain times and things rarely work out as planned. In fact, it could well be that I would make it worse than it is, even as I try to improve it, and I will be blamed for indulging myself in any case, since such subjects are more appropriate for young men than old ones. In fact, according to Petrarch in his canzone *Ben mi credea*,[57] all errors are more excusable in young people than in the maturity of old age. So for these and a thousand more reasons, all readily apparent to learned men, I have decided that I will receive much less shame if I send my work forth in Latin. For although many fewer people will understand it, among those some may be found who will find cocks, cunts, and assholes pleasing, and who might kiss my hands. And those who read only to criticize will bless it even more, for they will find much in the work to satisfy them, and they will be able to abundantly demonstrate the power of their wicked tongues. I have given them a lot to chew on. Thus, in this way, if either in the clumsiness or in the beauty of my work I bring delight to some literate man, that will be the height of pleasure for me; indeed my labors are not made to be placed in the hands of ignorant artisans, for whom I would not wish to give my sweat; for whenever I have ever asked them for the smallest thing, they have made me pay dearly for it.

I mourn, and will always mourn that those traitors,[58] to their great shame and ours, have made it so that every laborer and whore has all of Pliny, Livy, Ovid, Apuleius, and a thousand other excellent authors in their mouths. The other morning, I was watching a craftsman who was putting a lock on a strongbox, and I spoke with him about the welding of iron. "Have you ever seen Pliny," he asked me, "who wagers that he was the first to think of welding with a rasp?"[59] By God, I was ashamed of myself. Forget the welding of iron, which was his art, not mine. But when I asked him about the principles of welding, he gave me many more things that he had taken from Pliny, and in his discussion of the theory of welding he told me that fire came from water.[60] I'll tell you the truth, Sodo, when I heard him say that fire came from water I thought he was joking with me and I was ready to be really angry with him. But he quoted me Macrobius and Solinus,[61] and said so many things to me with such authority, that I pretended to believe him so I wouldn't seem to be an utter idiot. Afterward, when I looked it up, I found it all to be true, which made me want to throw out all my books— or burn them—and to stuff my fists up my ass and then strangle myself.

Why Learning Has Been Abandoned

It is the fault of these fools, ungrateful to the Latin language, that a locksmith who works with iron knows things that I don't, though I spend all day turning the pages of books? Discourteous people have thrown Latin into the gutter and thus have brought all use of Latin to hatred and disdain. And because of this, those who have no need to spend their time working to earn money to support themselves are ashamed to devote themselves to the study of Latin, since in ten years study they will barely learn the things a shoemaker can learn in a day.

Why No One Today Has Profound Knowledge

And if anyone devotes himself to study because he needs to earn his bread, you know he will never achieve anything worthwhile, because study should be a delight and not a necessity. Otherwise he will never seek to know more than what he needs to get some little thing he wants; and thus from the very outset, knowledge is parted from learning, and a liberal art is made a mechanic one.[62] This is why today one cannot find anyone who has profound knowledge, such as the ancients did.

Yet we find by experience that intelligent people today are all very subtle and refined. But if we want to consider rightly, the clever and subtle things in which we are wiser than the ancients all have to do with making money, dominating others, and similar things; and all depends on this, because wealth has placed its feet on virtue's neck. A man can have all the knowledge in the world, but if he has few worldly goods he is despised and seen as a fool. This is why the ancient philosophers were so critical of riches and the desire for wealth, because they knew that riches were the enemy of virtue. Virtue and Greed cannot exist together. And we can well see this is still true in our own time, for the rich and powerful hate the liberal arts more than a dog hates garlic.

Why Classical Philosophers Hated Wealth

From this I have sometimes thought that these traitors who translated Latin texts went around imagining that to overcome fortune, they would need to put their cocks in whatever hole they could—that is, they needed to teach virtue in a simpler way than would be necessary when teaching it to great men. And so they translate the great Latin works into this language of ours—though I would call Latin ours as much as Tuscan is, indeed much more so.[63] Therefore, although they took their alphabet from ours, the words and names of things were corrupted and were brought in from strangers living on

Why Latin Works Are Translated into the Vernacular

the other side of the Alps;[64] and although many excellent wits, recently aware of our many errors, have wearied themselves gathering words and adapting them,[65] nonetheless I believe that in a thousand places the language is ruined and changed. And I marvel that, although in Tuscany—the most beautiful place in all the world—there were always learned men, we find they were not able to establish rules and to find ways to preserve their language, as the Hebrews, Greeks, and Romans did. But in the past it was so ruined and pillaged by the Goths, Vandals, Huns, and other foreign and bestial peoples, summoned by our sins from the ends of the earth to come here and put everything to fire and sword. And yet this little bit of a language, which we have in such imperfect condition, has become so precious in these days that all nations desire it.[66] And I believe that when it is perfected, with its letters and its rules and measures, that it will be sweet and delightful. I would like very much for all Latin works to be translated into *that* Tuscan language, but a great deal of time will have to pass before that will be possible.

Therefore, it would please me if writers in these times, when they came to write their works, would write them in this sweet and pleasing Tuscan language, especially those of us who were born here. I believe that those who have written in this language up to now are worthy of great praise. But don't think that some idiots haven't grumbled about certain new words, like "sovente," "guari," "unqua," "maisempre," "altresì" and many other sweet, elegant, and proper terms the language has,[67] which—when they have been smoothly adapted to the language according to the proper rules—make such a sweet harmony of discourse that the authors themselves stand listening with their mouths open, like little sparrows waiting to be fed. It's true that some writers stretch the language, and change it so that it will fit the rules of rhyme: throwing in all sorts of things as if they were making a mixed salad, they create such harsh sounds and grating pronunciations that even dogs can't fit it in their mouths: If these writers end up getting bitten for it, who can complain? Because there is no one who can perfectly teach this language, we must seek high and low until we find the perfect harmony, just as people do when they tune musical instruments.[68] If I had planned to bring my writing closer to that sound, know that I would never write my work in Latin.

All the same, I tell you that a person who does not have good Latin cannot have a good command of Tuscan,[69] and the reason is this: Since Tuscan is not yet able to stand on its own feet,[70] and not yet having perfect proportions in itself, it must seek help from Latin things, and often discourses with the help of Latin wit, lines, and sweetness, and it must accommodate these things to itself as Latin did with Greek.[71] And for this reason, anyone who wants to penetrate the sweetness of the Tuscan language must enter by the Latin gate.

Sodo: Which one? The one in Rome?

Arsiccio: No, the one in Belforte![72] You want to joke, huh?

*Why
Common
People
Cannot
Understand
the Beauty
of the
Tuscan
Language*

This is why the vulgar cannot perceive the beauty of that speech, not knowing the Latin endings.

In any case it's bad to put things in people's hands if they don't understand them and don't know what to do with them, and for this reason I didn't want to put all those cocks in the hands of a bunch like that. And because they wouldn't understand it even if they knew how to read it, I wrote it in Latin. Besides it is a fairly long work, and those with other things to do would soon find it tedious. But the thing that most induced me to write about the cock in Latin is that way only learned men would read it. And even though it is a shameful book, it would not make their habits any worse than they are. Nor would they condemn me, knowing that Ovid, Apulieus, and other Romans wrote at length about the art of fucking, and Martial, Horace, and Virgil wrote about cocks;[73] they will judge that since I am a lesser writer than these are, it is more permissible for me to write about the circumstances surrounding the cock. If I had written the book for the vulgar instead of for the learned, I would have been forced to demonstrate all these things in a long introduction. Nor indeed can anyone who wants to remove cocks, cunts, or other things less natural and honest from my work tear up the book, since I here have ordered that it should be burned and torn in pieces before it might give others in any pleasant way that which I have written in it, however good or bad it may be.

Indeed, let anyone read it who wants to, for they'll get nothing out of it, except that it's Nature that teaches us to fuck. And if anyone should be blamed, it's her, who gave us cocks, cunts, and assholes, and taught us all sorts of other hateful things. And so that everyone could see it and know it, we were made naked. But neither she, nor I, nor anyone else who teaches these things ought to be condemned. For if we teach and speak well about ugly things we do not force or command anyone to do them who doesn't want to, but let those who can be pleased by them take them and taste them. You may do likewise with the things I plan to tell you tonight: don't think I tell you these things I tell you because I am looking for the chance to say or do something foolish. But I want you to know this, so that, when you need to, like tonight, you will know it, and you will be able to use it dexterously. For you should know that the ability to make and concoct poisons is greatly valued and honored, and this is why Pietro d'Abbano[74] is so highly praised. Nor indeed do I teach you these things, Sodo, so that you can impress people by showing how much you know about them; indeed, however good many things might be, it is nonetheless not always good to use them too much or too often—as is the case with wine and many many other things. And so I have learned to swim, not for exercise, but to save my life if I need to. In short, it seems that it is better to know our art than to adopt it, even though often knowledge without the ability to act on it brings little or no joy. And I have just now experienced the same thing, because even though I know that drinking helps one to talk, nevertheless, since I'm not drinking I'm not taking pleasure in it, even though I know that I could ask for some to chase away the dryness in my throat.

Sodo: Ha! Ha! Yes, yes, I understand—you would like a drink, eh?

Arsiccio: That's it, my wise Sodo, by God! I think few men could have understood me right away like that, just as you did. Indeed I'm dying of thirst, and if you think I'm going to babble away all night with a dry mouth, you're very much mistaken. Anyway, it seems to me that here in our nightshirts we might drink a sip or two, and it will have the best effects: firstly, according to Tivizzano we won't fall asleep so quickly, and as well, as Sosperone Intronato[75] says, we'll also speak more clearly. And when we *are* ready to sleep we'll fall asleep more quickly, as Ippocrates the Fat Pig says in verse 6000.13 of his *Palette.*[76] You know that without the help of Bacchus one can't speak about cocks as well as one ought to.

Sodo: By God, you're right, Arsiccio. I remember a phrase from Ovid which ought to be written in letters of adamantine: *Sine Cerere et Bacco friget Venus.*[77]

Arsiccio: That's it! That's it! Ah, good, that's settled then. So go get some wine.

Sodo: Here it is, good and ready! Drink as much as you like! Now snuggle up and begin at the place you left off.

Arsiccio: Come on, now, Sodo. Don't interrupt me with my cock here next to your ass, at least not until I've got what I want.

Sodo: I get it. Now go ahead.

Arsiccio: In my reading of ancient and modern texts, I learn that violent tyranny has never lasted long, or brought any profit to those who sought it. Indeed I often find that the fall of such regimes is greater and quicker than their rise. Nor, it seems, is tyranny content to take all delights and noble honors from men and to return them to their primal state; indeed, it never rests until their adversaries are sunk in the profoundest misery, with all goods taken from them. If the Cocks of whom I intend to speak[78] had well understood this they might have followed a civil and honorable way of life, respecting others as much as themselves, enjoying companionship, honor, and reputation without harm, in the favorable and peaceful state which their fortune or industry had earned them. And they might still be held today to be upright and in great repute, and they might be caressed, openly seen, and welcomed by Cunts, Assholes, and every courteous person; they would not go miserably dispersed throughout the world, exiled and hated for their vanity. And this is the main reason why, not without cause, they are often depicted holding their eyes and ears closed with their hands so they will not see or hear anything unpleasant. Fooling themselves in this manner, they cannot see justice, which consists only in considering the good of others equally with one's own. The power to command and be obeyed is so sweet and pleasing that there are few today who are able to rule without worrying about the consequences, and they do it unwillingly.

So I'm not surprised at these Cocks, who are mere animals, when I see all the most learned men of our time study nothing else but tyrannical power. But in those ancient times, as Livy writes in his second *Decade*,[79] the Cocks, like all the other bodily members, were sentient and knew all about government, and they reigned industriously. Of all the members, the Cocks, being the most practiced and involved in things, knew how to control the hands so well that many of them became grand and powerful and were held in most respect by the other members. As is always the case, those who sit well think badly—and thus it was with them. It was not enough for them to have all the gifts fortune could give them. It was not enough for them that Nature had given them the most favorable appearance possible, and had made them magnificent—they began to think of making themselves masters and of ruling the other members. So they decided it would be useful to corrupt the Cunts and make them submit to their desires, and thus to bear their strength in hand. And this was accomplished all too easily, for the Cunts, naturally disdainful of Little Cocks, quickly fell in line with the Big Cocks to raise themselves to the ruling class, thinking the Big Cocks would favor them in the state and hold them in esteem.

Once the Big Cocks came to power with the favor of the Cunts, they elected a chief from among themselves, who took the name and sign of a tyrant, and was called "the great." They placed him on a throne, and he held the scepter of the state in his hands. This Cazzone[80] began to rule very cruelly. His first plan was to turn against his own kind and hold them in subjection and milk them for all they were worth. Thus he took away all the access and honors and all the public offices from the hands of the Little Cocks and distributed them among his allies the Big Cocks and the Cunts, so that in no time at all the tiny Little Cocks had fallen so low and were held in such disdain that not only other Cocks, but even the Cunts despised and scorned them. Their little heads hung down on their shoulders. Resigned to their sorry state, they consoled themselves as best they could, and made every effort to become friends with the Assholes, who at that time, finding themselves mistreated by the Big Cocks, were happy to ally themselves with the Little Cocks.

They began to hold secret meetings among themselves and many times spoke openly about getting themselves out from under such a bestial government. However, because they were weaker than the Big Cocks and all the Cunts, they saw no way to fulfill their plans. But Heaven, just observer of good works and severe judge of evil deeds, gave a great opportunity to their plots. For it often happens that princes and great men at the height of their success neglect and torment those who first raised them to high office, people who, even though they are small, are still able to be of great service. Sometimes to twist out of the obligation they have from the benefits they received—which they do not wish to repay— they even have their benefactors killed. Thus it was with the ungrateful Big Cocks. When their rule was endangered, and they had needed all the help they could get, they stroked all the Cunts they could. But once they saw themselves securely installed in power, they no longer worried about any threats because they had solidified and consolidated their rule. And they began to treat the Ugly Cunts the same way they had earlier treated the Little Cocks—driving them out and torturing them shamefully. And thus the wretched Cunts became aware of their error too late, and they experienced to their great harm just how wrong they were to come between the Cocks, putting the large ones on top and turning on the little ones. And so—as they deserved—they found themselves hated all at once by both sides: The Little Cocks, knowing that they were rejected and set aside by the Cunts, grew so hostile toward them that their hatred endures to this day and they avoid them whenever possible. And the Big Cocks, who had become proud after their rise to power, did not believe they would ever need the Cunts again, and held them to be no better than putrid carrion. The Big Cocks favored and valued only the Beautiful Cunts.

Sodo: I had never heard, Arsiccio, that there were two kinds of Cunts—that is, beautiful and ugly ones.

Arsiccio: I'm not surprised, Sodo, since I see that you are ignorant of many other things, some of which are more important than this.

Sodo: Come on! Don't get upset. I'll know it as soon as you tell me about it. But please, Arsiccio, I would be delighted if you could tell me how both the Beautiful Cunts and the ugly ones are made, and what their characteristics are.

Arsiccio: They have a red ribbon[81]—haven't you ever noticed it?

Sodo: Not me. Where do they keep it?

Arsiccio: Up their ass.

Sodo: Tell me the truth!

Arsiccio: I'm afraid, Sodo, that you're trying to make a fool of me.[82]

Sodo: Why?

Arsiccio: What do you mean, "why"? Oh, you say some things that would never come out of the mouth of an oven.[83] By God, how can you believe that women have red ribbons?

Sodo: Oh, so you say it, but you don't want me to believe it?

Arsiccio: And if I were to tell you next that donkeys fly, you'd believe that too, eh?

Sodo: Fine! Fine! Whatever you like. Hey, slow down, I'm not quite as dumb as all that. By the devil, it's too much. You take me for a very simple person, but I want you to understand that I scarcely believe all these things you swear are true. Don't think—with all the things you've told me—that I just believe everything you say.

Arsiccio: Now that I understand rightly, if you don't believe all that I've told you up to now about the cock, the cunt, and the asshole, these are nonetheless things you can touch with your hand and can easily test for yourself and know through experience. Know that it's just as foolish to not believe something that is demonstrably true as it is to believe something you know to be impossible. Now it is true that all I've told you so far about cocks and cunts you are not able to witness for yourself, because these events are so distant and ancient that you will find no one who remembers them. But if we want to believe the things we find written down, there is no matter so large or deeply studied in all authors than this business of the Cunts: that is, that there were two kinds of them—beautiful and ugly. But if you don't want to believe it, then I don't want to keep on talking for nothing—you can just go off and sleep.

Sodo: Arsiccio, you're getting upset over nothing.

Arsiccio: No, no, I know what you're like. You say at first that you won't interrupt me. And then no sooner than I've started but you break in and make me get into a tangle of Cocks that even Saint Francis couldn't find his way out of. And you pull me so far from what I was saying that just to get back in takes an enormous amount of time and energy. If the night were long I'd let you say whatever you wanted to, but it's short, and it's already after midnight. I have so much left to tell you that I'll hardly have any time to sleep. So tonight let me say whatever I want to, and then, if you still have any doubts, ask me about them another time, because you're always asking me about certain things that will be made clear to you in a little while—like your question about Beautiful Cunts. So wait until I've given you the whole discourse, and afterward, if you

see that I haven't given you every detail, ask about it then—
otherwise you'll get everything out of order. So if you want
to sit quietly I'll go on. If not, I have no desire to talk about
Cocks and all these other things in a disorderly fashion.

Sodo: You're right, Arsiccio. Go on. I won't say another word,
unless you ask me to.

Arsiccio: As I was saying, when the Cunts found themselves
despised by the Big Cocks, they thought of ways to avenge
themselves. So they found one of their group called the Cunt
of Modena,[84] who was wise and prudent, complaining to
certain Little Cocks, lamenting the wrong Cazzone had done
her. She had for a long time been his lover, but he abandoned
her for a Cunt called Snatch, who was highly esteemed by
other Beautiful Cunts. As they talked further, they soon realized that they all longed to destroy the Big Cocks. Thus
weeping they opened up to each other, and promised that
when it came time to do the thing they planned, they would
wipe out all the Beautiful Cunts as well, and they would use
all their energies to bring their plans to fruition. They agreed
that they should tell certain other Cocks, and she should
speak to certain other Cunts, and they arranged that on the
following day they should get together with the most important ones in some designated place, where they hoped to
gather together many Cocks and there they could hold a
more lengthy parliament. Above all they warned each other
that everything should be done in secret.

The next day with perfect organization, in a certain little wood not far from the city about seventy Cocks—the best of the little ones—gathered together with a similar number of Ugly Cunts. After long speeches and deep laments, in which with great rancor they rehearsed all the cruelties they had suffered from the Big Cocks, they all came together in union and brotherhood, promising each other that they would sacrifice their goods and their lives for the common good. They swore to kill and destroy all the Big Cocks, along with the Beautiful Cunts, their lovers and favorites. They thought of raising the people in rebellion, rushing suddenly into the houses and killing everyone they found. But they knew themselves to be weaker than their enemies and doubted they would be able to accomplish their goals as easily as they hoped. So they decided they should meet with the Assholes, whom they knew to be the natural enemies of the Big Cocks. And soon they cleverly thought of going to their friends and allies the Balls, and asking them to lend a hand in their undertaking. With this resolution agreed on, they kissed each other on the mouth and left the woods. They returned to the city—Cocks in one group, Cunts in the other—and they knew so well how to handle and deal with the Balls and Assholes that in a few days they were all great friends.

When it seemed the right time to tell them their plans, they called them all together in a certain secret place. There they lamented the extent of their calamity and cursed the violent government of the Big Cocks, who had made themselves rulers by force, not just over the Cunts and Little Cocks, but also over the Balls and Assholes. They told the Balls and Assholes they would rather die than live under such a cruel and bestial regime. And so, too, they wanted the Balls and Assholes to help them accomplish their goal and to all join together; they offered to organize both government and society on a legal and participatory basis, and they offered to be friends and brothers—and if the Balls and Assholes still didn't want to help them regain their lost liberties they should simply let them do what they could by themselves and only give them their moral support. In short, whatever might happen, they were decided and ready to go into action.

The Assholes were a proud and magnanimous people, whom, since they hated living in subjugation, replied that they thought the reconquest of their liberty from the Big Cocks was as much their struggle as it was for the Little Cocks or the Ugly Cunts. And besides, they had this in their favor—they wanted to break the heavy yoke of the tyranni-cal government through their own force and effort. They had long thought of this themselves, and were only waiting for the right moment to act. So if anyone wanted to unite with them, they would help them as much as possible—it would be a great pleasure. This promised, they laid forth their thoughts on the subject: they said that whoever was commit-ted to the common good would be honored by them and respected and valued according to their merits, and on the other hand, whoever did not want to follow their plan would be held as a mortal enemy, and would be treated accordingly. In conclusion, if the Cunts and Cocks wanted to tear things up with one hand, the Assholes were ready with both hands, and every hour that action was delayed seemed like a thou-sand years to them.

It remained for the Balls to speak. When the Balls heard the Assholes talk so boastfully, and saw that the Cocks, Cunts, and Assholes were all in strong agreement, they said they too were of the same opinion, even though they were very upset with the plans. It remained only to choose a time at which the plans could be put into effect. Meanwhile they had to make it clear to everyone gathered there that it was not until that certain day at a certain hour that they should get together with their weapons in their hands to wreak ruin and destruction on the Big Cocks. Their agreement was believed by everyone; no one saw the ill will that can be hidden behind beautiful flowery words. So they all decided that at the solemn festival which was soon to be held, when the Big Cocks and the Beautiful Cunts would go in a group to visit the temple of Burning Lust at the time when the apples ripen, just then they should rush into the house of Cazzone with weapons in their hands and kill him and his followers, as well as the Beautiful Cunts, and sack the house. Once they had agreed to the plan and sworn to put it into effect, they left in great happiness, awaiting with great anticipation the established resolution of their problems. Thus incited, the Ugly Cunts, the Little Cocks, and the Assholes would themselves be the instrument to bring down the great and bestial Big Cocks.

At that time the Balls, by nature timid and fearful, fond of peace and quiet, reconsidered the plan, and it seemed a horrible thing to them to cause displeasure to anyone. They thought of removing themselves from the plot; and finally they went along to the Big Cocks and told them how their overthrow had been planned and ordained. When the Big Cocks heard all this, they and the Beautiful Cunts mobilized their forces against the conspirators and assaulted them with the great forces they summoned together, killing a great number and capturing still more, whom they afflicted with various torments.

They tightened up many of the Assholes, so that they could never more join with a cock in any manner. And so it is that their descendants still today are called tightasses because just as those whose member is not apt and ready to do that which commonly all men can do are said to be uptight, so those Assholes who cannot enjoy the natural and common benefit of taking a cock are called tightasses, and are not at all esteemed by us.

Why People Who Can't Take It Up the Ass Are Called Uptight

But all this was nothing compared to what was done to the Ugly Cunts at the instigation of the wicked Beautiful Cunts. Besides the many that were killed, others were taken, ripped up, ruptured, torn, and thrown in muck and slime so that from that time forth they could never wash or clean themselves and they would always smell like rotten flesh and putrid carrion. It is said that the Devil once tried to wash one at the mouth of the Po River, and to make a long story short, he had no success, for on the last day she smelled as bad as she had on the first.

Why Cunts Can Never Be Washed So Well They Lose Their Smell

Cugino nell'Intronato[85] says that the herring was born from this stink, for when passing a woman in San Martino[86] Street in Siena she said "this smells like us." And the clamor and destruction of the miserable creatures were so great that they would never be Cunts again, and began to be slits and

Why Herring Smell Like Cunts

snatches and other filthy, reeking things. Worse, the Beautiful Cunts sliced them right across their mustaches, and so if you look at them nose to nose you will see that to this day they all bear a great wound, which was either made with a poisoned blade or poorly treated by the doctors. Or perhaps the Big Cocks left them like that to mark their eternal shame, which seems more likely.

Why Women Have Periods   Their wound was never able to heal, indeed it became infected, and they became—so to speak—lunatic, for their wounds were renewed each new moon. And from this comes that flow of blood which they call their "period" or "curse," which truly is nothing more than a purge of their malignant infected wound. And that is why this blood is so noxious to everything and greatly harms anything that it touches, because it still retains the nature of the original poison.

In this way the Little Cocks, the Assholes, and the Cunts were punished by the Big Cocks who, affected by their disdain, began to rule even more severely, and exerted their tyrannical reign without any pity or compassion. They entered by force, now into a cunt, now into an asshole, so that in a few days they ruled them all. There is no heart so hard that, seeing at that time those poor Little Cocks and those miserable Assholes—filthy, beaten up, mistreated, and covered in shit—would not have cried for pity. And they would also have pitied the massacre and anguish, the extortions, the injustices decreed in public assemblies, and other infinite torments inflicted on the wretched and unfortunate Ugly Cunts. Beaten, broken, filthy, frightened, branded, and stinking, they hid themselves as best they could. For they were ashamed to show themselves openly to any man. And there was no one so ugly of body or wicked in spirit that, seeing their calamity and their disgusting secretions, did not avert his eyes, and it was only with difficulty that he could keep from vomiting his guts out.

So do not marvel if these unfortunate creatures are still ashamed to be uncovered to this day and never let themselves be seen clearly, in order to hide a profound abyss and horrible cavern, their dishonorable pit and dark ditch, in which they were placed by the strange and bestial Big Cocks.

Why Cunts Are Kept Hidden

Indeed, I should not wish you to marvel at their great size and bestial capacity, for today they have gotten no worse, but it seems as if our cocks barely touch the edges of the immense and omnipotent cunt. Indeed, Folletico Intronato[87] replied wisely when he was asked where the bottom of the cunt could be found. For he said it was the depth of the palm of one's hand, which—if placed in a woman's mouth—will just reach to the bottom of the cunt. That is to say, the cunt reaches all the way to the mouth, because it was knocked through like that by those Big Cocks I told you about.

Why Cunts Are So Big

Similarly, it can also be proved that the asshole reaches all the way to the mouth, because if you put something in your mouth it eventually comes out of your ass. It is because of this, as Affumicato Intronato[88] maintains, that one kisses by putting one's tongue into another's mouth, in an attempt to feel if the cock has gone in all the way. This opinion is tested by Svegliato Intronato,[89] in his *Civil Wars between the Cats and Mice* (which he has written). Around the middle of the

Why We Kiss with the Tongue when Fucking

book he says that cocks cannot enter the asshole unless they know how to use a little trick, and it is the tongue that will teach them this. It is done with saliva, which the tongue uses to get between the teeth.

Why Kissing Feels Good

So by this expedient the cock and the asshole are brought together, and this is why the cock, the asshole, and the cunt all take part in the pleasure that one feels with the tongue while fucking. And the tongue is obliged, when fucking, to help the cock with any saliva it needs. "And that this is true," he says, "can be seen because kissing with the tongue is good even if you aren't fucking, which would not be the case if Affumicato was right."

I would demonstrate that these opinions are far from the truth, if I did not hear the clamorous racket the Little Cocks, the Cunts, the Assholes, the Big Cocks, and the Beautiful Cunts were making. For the Assholes, no longer able to bear the harsh blows and cruel pricks the Big Cocks were giving them, and not wanting to take it any longer, gathered themselves together, and decided either to die or to deliver themselves from such troubles. They raised the people, and as closely and quietly as could be they raced to Cazzone's house. Finding him with certain other Big Cocks and certain Beautiful Cunts who had come together to consult among themselves, they killed him and all his companions. From there they ran to the houses of the others, and as many as they found they put to the point of the sword. And because some of the Big Cocks hearing the outcry had retreated to certain fortified places, it took a long time and much effort to storm them, and many died on both sides. Now I do not need to tell you that the Ugly Cunts pushed themselves passionately in front of the bastions in order to elevate themselves and overcome such despairing and dishonorable Cocks, nor about the torments they inflicted on them. In short, they stormed them with the greatest possible slaughter; they did not rest until all the Big Cocks were cut down, and as far as anyone can tell very few escaped, and those only with great difficulty. This was not the case for the Beautiful Cunts, for, being cowardly women and badly suited for flight, they were all killed and wiped out. In fact, from that day to this no one has ever seen one and few have even mentioned them. No memory of their appearance remains.

It is true that, as Ombroso Intronato[90] says, in the days when Beffania held the dukedom of Archifanfano di Baldracca in Aldalecca, on Giudecca near the Yellow Sea[91] a stone was found on which was sculpted from life a Big Cock and a Cunt. They were very different in form from those which we see today, but it was thought that the cunt was one of those beautiful ones: it rose from a rounded and elevated pubes with a few curly hairs around it, crisp and firm, very similar to the asshole of a beautiful young man. From this came a great dispute between Brother Buio,[92] the excellent architect, and Scannaconfetti,[93] a philosopher of that age, both wondering whether it was an Asshole or a Cunt. Finally they concluded that it was a beautiful cunt, of a shape which need not concern us at the moment, since we know that today they've been wiped out, root and branch.

As far as the Big Cocks are concerned, as I told you, it was thought that some had escaped. People said they were as long as a footstep, and of unequal width up to the head—in a pyramidal form, larger at the base, with bands on them like ribs. The head made up a quarter of the whole length, and bulged out more than two fingers' width, with a deep and definite notch. And this notch, according to Impassionato Intronato[94] was made in the cock so to hold back the foreskin when the cock entered into some cunt or asshole. The foreskin was intended to cover the head, so that no ugly thing might ruin the soft smoothness that makes it so penetrating. In this it agrees with the tables in old books, and I believe it. But to this day I have never yet found a woman or man who has ever seen in our own time a cock that could be called big, so I don't know if I believe this account or not. Let it go. There's no time to argue about it now.

But I tell you, to return to our story, the force of the Cocks, the rage of the Cunts, and the fury of the Assholes was so great that they did not stop until they saw the cruel Big Cocks and the proud and disdainful Beautiful Cunts smashed, ruined, dead, and flattened. They found many of them hidden in sepulchres, in cellars, in wells, and in other dark, ugly places, for there was no hole that the Little Cocks didn't enter. Their anger was so great that some of them at last began to search even in shit, and some were stuck there and stayed there. You may well believe that those who fell into the hands of the Assholes were treated just as they deserved. So in such a manner they recovered their lost liberty, and cast out the great tyrants.

After their victory, in order to bring rule and order to their state, they wanted to live well with well-established government of the best type that might be—a government that would make peace, observe justice, and maintain a unified state. So, laying down their arms, the Cocks, Assholes, and Cunts all assembled in the senate, and began a series of debates to choose a leader or group of leaders who should hold power. It seemed that the majority were agreed in wanting a leader elected from among their number, but there was great dissention over which group he should come from and each group wanted to elect one of their own. There were harsh words, and they began to shout and to divide into parties: both the Cocks and Cunts felt strongly that they had had the greatest part in the seizure of the state, and it seemed to each of them that if any group should be privileged, it should be them. The Assholes, on the other hand, grumbled that they had suffered more, and stipulated that the government should not be taken out of their hands. But the Cunts had a different opinion: they proposed that a communal state should be established, and they believed that they were better suited to rule than the Assholes were. Because if there had to be a leader, arrogance, pride, disdain, and self-interest—all characteristic of Cocks and Assholes—were the certain enemies of justice, responsibility, and civic life. Whereas, being by nature humble, magnanimous, and generous, the Cunts seemed more apt than any other group for the task at hand. Besides, they were physically weak, and likely to be overthrown if they ever governed badly (which would not happen to the thriving Cocks or the proud and disdainful Assholes; if they ruled badly once they got the government into their hands it would not be so easy to take it out of their hands). It seemed there was no good reason to take power away from the Cunts. Realizing this, the Assholes and Cocks came up with an alternative plan, and with much shuddering they began to shout and turn the meeting upside down.

Seeing this, Cazzatello,[95] a very honest, wise, and moderate Cock, who had been the first and principal Cock to throw out the Big Cocks, quickly leaped to his feet, and motioning for silence with his head, spoke to them all in this way:

"Honorable brothers and sisters! I believe that experience has shown you that nothing is so contrary to universal peace and well-being than discord, the origin and cause of all ruin in civil and political life. I also think that the tortures, cruelties, and anguish you suffered under the tyrants' yoke have taught you to search out by force or wit, with your goods and with your blood to extinguish and crush every root from which the plague of tyranny could shoot forth— roots such as self-interest, ambition, hatred and rancor, supremacy, pride, singularity, and infinite other wicked vices. Now, from what I can see, you are acting as if you had always lived free in this happy state, and you had never had any experience of misery: The first day that you've had any power and a chance to act, you have given yourselves over to dissension, to ambitious desire for rule, not realizing—you miserable people—how serious our situation is, how much trouble is looming, and how much danger we're in. I am so sorry to see you this way that I would rather that I had been killed at the rude hands of the Big Cocks than to live to see you in the sad state I see you in now. The office of leadership is rejected by wise men because, while it may be sweet and useful to others, it brings nothing but trouble and care to the one who bears it. When I see every one of you wanting above all to rule the others, I cannot think but that you are all seeking universal disaster. At the same time, I regret that fortune did not let me die in yesterday's tumult; then with more glory and happiness I might have given my members back to Nature—finally free. And then I would not be grieving to see your mistakes today. I beg you, if you have set your hearts on following these evil plans of yours, that the first thing you do may be to take my life from me, and I will bless the pious hand that brings me such content. But if you want to live well, as you demonstrated yesterday with such a glorious beginning, and if my words have any meaning for you, if my mature age or long experience can teach you anything, make your first great work that of concord and union, from which come all benefits and which maintain all good things. Dispose yourselves to study justice, the mother and origin of all noble and honorable work, which consists in a just dispensation according to the merits of each one of you. And thus you may put ambition and self-interest aside, and none of you will believe that his own good must include the punishment of others. And from this must necessarily come peace and the establishment of a tranquil and happy state.

"The establishment of justice and stabilization of government can be accomplished in one of three ways.[96] First and most perfect is that in which one leader governs, like God in Heaven, or the father in the household, just as among bees, one is chosen to arrange the distribution of tasks and to set the schedule for carrying them out. As I know this is not an option for us, there is no need to discuss it further. The second way is for a group of men to be chosen to lead—and it is worse than the first because among the leaders the evil seed of discord may flourish, which cannot happen if there is only one ruler. The last, and worst of all, is uncertain and universal government, where the fools have as much authority to judge as the wise do, because in many cases they will tend toward things full of ignorance. Besides, this is more dangerous than the two other forms, because it is most accessible to all, as we have seen today. And yet, seeing that we are of three species, we cannot have just one head. But it is nonetheless necessary, so that we don't fall into the worst government possible, that from each group we elect a certain number of people who, once chosen, will have the authority to unite us and guide us as they please, and everyone should obey them. Those elected should hold office for a set time, which I believe would best be the remainder of their lives, since there is nothing that teaches us how to live better than experience, and that cannot be acquired except over time. Thus it follows that a temporary term will not be able to provide complete experience of the office; it is as if a man were deprived of a teacher just as he was learning. All the same, if an elected official acts against the will of the electors, when offices are temporary, he can be replaced, which cannot happen if they are perpetual, in which case they will perpetuate bad government. Nonetheless, in this matter I will let those more experienced than I am counsel you. And I beg you to have your best interests at heart and that you live in unity, and it is certain that if you do not do this, first you will please your enemies, then with your ruin you will ensure their greatness, and you will return again to your past miseries."

After these words Cazzatello fell silent, and his wise counsels pleased everyone. His effective reasoning had such power that many Cocks and many Cunts, crying with tenderness, began to put aside their pride, making themselves humble and meek. The Assholes, for their part, sighed with compassion at the beautiful and affectionate words of Cazzatello, to which they had listened with open-mouthed attention—it seemed that the wind had gone out of them. They greatly praised his prudent speech and it seemed that there was universal agreement to elect representatives, as he had suggested, from each group—that is, as many Cocks as Cunts and Assholes—and then to give them full authority over the administration of the state.

But then Albagio,[97] a Cock of bad reputation and worse habits, thought that if things were arranged the way Cazzatello had suggested, he would always remain someone of no account, so he wanted to see if he could create some discord in order to put things in a mess. All flustered and red in the face, poking out from behind certain Assholes where up to now he had been lying in wait, he leaped up on the rostrum to give himself some distance from the other Cocks and Cunts standing around him, and, removing his hood, began to speak these words against Cazzatello:

"Even though you Assholes and Cocks have often thought of me as crude and almost bestial in nature, lacking both wit and judgment, nonetheless I am not so stupid that

I don't see my own destruction and the destruction of all you other Cocks, if you will let yourselves be taken in hand and corrupted by these Cunts and these Assholes, and to be brought low by their seeming kindness. Do not think that I am presumptuous or that I am speaking arrogantly, for I want to convince these older Cocks, who don't believe that others can see things that they can't. Nor do they think that when they have failed to figure something out with all their wits, that there is anyone else in the world who can figure it out. I am still young, I'm not even old enough to wear a cap on my head, and I don't spend all day thinking deep thoughts with my head hung down like this, but nevertheless, in matters of universal interest I know how to look out for myself, and for all of you. Besides being able to make good decisions, I have also shown myself to be strong; with the work of my hands I have worn myself out bringing your plans to fruition. So when it comes to installing or removing Cunts and Assholes from the government, it seems fitting to me that I should look out for my own advantage. Furthermore, seeing that all of you seem to have decided to favor the establishment of justice, I am forced to remind you that, through ignorance, you might decide something which goes against any standard of justice. Simply put, the ideas that Cazzatello put forth and you all agreed to, are the greatest possible error. It seems to me a great injustice that, although we Cocks have always ruled over the Cunts and Assholes, now we should abase ourselves to become equal with them. Nor do I want the evil deeds of the Big Cocks, who thrashed us other Cocks far worse than they did you others, should harm us by ensuring that now that they have been thrown out, we will not be able to reclaim our traditional authority. Nor do I wish that you brag about your deeds, even if they were great and important. However important, they should not lead to this result. For you Cunts and you Assholes worked to overthrow the proud Big Cocks not because you wanted to rule, for you did not seize power, but to escape the torments and violence they wreaked upon you. As for us, both when each group rose up in revolt against them, and now when they have been chased out, the right of rulership falls to us by reason of just succession. All the same, I do not believe that you should be cast down as if you had been subjugated and overcome by force, since your good actions are worthy of the highest praise and do not merit such a fate. But I want the one chosen to be our magistrate to be of equal condition with us Cocks, equally honored and revered, otherwise I see that in order to escape from servitude I have placed my very life in danger. This is my plan for the future. And whoever disagrees with me in this, plans to take the very life from me. In any case it would not be worth living under an unjust government, which is what we will have if anyone other than a Cock is entrusted with the rulership and administration of the state."

Albagio the Cock had barely finished speaking before a rumbling was heard through all the senate—a strong threatening shudder from the Assholes and the grinding of the lips of the Cunts. For the proud and disdainful words of that bestial, obscene Cock Albagio had greatly upset both groups. They were already about to punish his great hatred or die taking up the struggle against the proud and treacherous Cock. He, persevering in his treachery with an evil disposition, had moved to one side with some of his followers gathered around him. For his spirit would not let him rest from taking up arms to combat the Cunts and Assholes, so that, dead or alive, he might see them brought down.

At this, many Cocks, who wanted to live well, gathered together with certain Cunts, and with raised voices they motioned to stop the quarrel and diffuse the evil situation. Among them, the wise old Cunt of Modena, her mouth wide open, cried out in the following manner: "Hey, for God's sake listen to me, and stop your fighting, at least until I've shown my own feelings to you, mine and all the other Cunts'. I want you by the grace of God to realize what a good and happy state you find yourselves in, and I don't want the ill-considered words of that Cock Albagio to be the cause of your ultimate ruin. Perhaps if he had known what I mean to say to you he would not have rushed into his own strange speech—as he did—and you would not have all been so upset by the words of one person. And indeed, if Heaven was always gracious to you, you would be pleased to hear my plan, which I hope will bring about concord and universal unity, and the contentment and well-being of all."

At the outcry and the speech of the great Cunt of Modena, the anger of the Assholes dissipated, and they embraced all the Cocks—and already they fell silent to hear what she would say. Seeing them give her such respectful audience, and after seeing several of them standing very still with their eyes cast down, deep in thought, she let forth a deep sigh and, raising her eyes to Heaven, opened her mouth and spoke these words: "I truly believe that no misery is so great today as this disorder that is gripping you. This vice is common to all victors. For after they have, with much danger and much sweat, come through fire and ice to get what they desire, just when they should be most peaceful and united, they become mortal enemies. Many times I have seen victory bring more ruin and destruction to those who win than to those who were overcome. And the wisest people believe this happens because of the pestiferous root and cruel enemy of all peace—sad and abominable pride, which has such a wicked nature and which is so strong against reason that philosophers have called it an indestructible beast.

"And so it is said, and very truly, that nothing is so praiseworthy as to conquer oneself—that is to overthrow the depraved and unjust tyranny of the arrogant spirit, which can be overcome with no other weapon than humility, the mother and guardian of all just government, and the clear and open way to arrive at the true light of reason. But I do not believe that you have won by having overthrown tyranny and recaptured your lost liberty, because as I told you the most important part of true victory is the casting out of pride and presumption from oneself, disposing oneself not to judge, but to be judged. For from self-interested judgment and the bestial belief that anyone other than yourself must be weaker comes this cursed pride, so hated by God, that raises itself so high that there is no hill, or city, or tower, or mountain so sublime that can be found that pride cannot topple, ruin, and abase it, and throw it down to earth. And

Why It Is Praiseworthy to Control Oneself

there has never been any state built on law, custom, high glory, or any stable and well-founded republic that has not very quickly transformed itself into a cruel, horrible, and hateful den of thieves. To give you a better understanding of this most powerful of all vices and its evil effects, pride is not only enemy to all good actions, it brings even greater harm to the proud themselves. There has never been a proud person who has not very quickly come to a bad end. For a clear and recent sign of this, you can take the final ruin and slaughter of those great Big Cocks, of which you yourselves were the virile and magnanimous cause. Since I certainly love all of you, and since we Cunts all have a great love for both Cocks and Assholes, and since we even have sexual desires for you, we can only greatly lament anything that would diminish our communal comfort and well-being. And yet, knowing that ambition has entered into you, ambition, rancor, and arrogant disdain, think of how it breaks our hearts to consider how much evil may come of this. So to show you how great our goodwill is toward you and to show you the way to free yourselves from the grip of pride with the help of humility—all the more since the greatness of us Cunts is traditionally deep beyond measure, and we have always contributed (as far as is known), both before and behind, to the building of the scepter and government of Black Mountain,[98] nevertheless—considering the present danger and the threat of ruin, we have arranged to abase and humble ourselves, seeing the burden that is before us. And if the Cocks have any bad blood or disdain between them and the Assholes, they should turn to us, and vent it all on us.

Similarly, if you Assholes desire anything, tell us what it is you want. So that peace and concord will follow, carry yourselves any way you like, in any case we are ready and prepared to please you, whether it concerns state business or anything else that weighs on you, if you, following our example, will leave your arrogance, settle your dissention, and think of making your victory a true and complete one. Do not feed your appetite for gain and for acquiring things, for this will finish you off even if you do nothing else besides. Such greed can still bring you grief and suffering. Thus it is, if you do not extirpate all the roots of evil, in a short time you will see them grow and multiply in their wicked effects.

"I will say this about the Big Cocks, few of whom survive today: It is very possible that they have taken refuge with some foreign power, from where in a short time, seeing our discord, they may return to ruin and destroy each of us. And indeed, before waiting for anything else, I think we ought to consider wiping out their seed, and in my judgment I believe nothing more apt for this or more quick to make them enemies than our promising to give gold to anyone who meets them and kills them. For you know that against gold neither constancy of spirit, nor firm resolution, nor loyal faith, nor promises given, nor chaste thoughts, nor bonds of friendship, nor habits of virtue are sufficient. It would take a long time to tell how much power gold holds in the hearts of men and the strength it has to make everything seem the way you want it to be. And indeed, if we put this bell on them, wherever they may go, people will want to kill them, and soon they will be either dead or driven away; that is, it will be nec-

essary for them to go so far away that we will never hear any
news of them. In this way, all the fear we have of them will
be transferred and they will fear us instead. Wherever they go
they will fear a thousand things—and this fear will be
enough all on its own to send them to their deaths, since they
were accustomed to tranquil rest and a soft life of privilege.

"After this, in order to annihilate every last seed of those
who hurt you or who could threaten you in the future, it is
necessary that you find some way to punish these obscene,
scurrilous, and wicked Balls, the vilest wretches of all, who as
the worst truly malignant traitors were the cause of our greatest suffering. I feel that no penalty could be atrocious and horrible enough to punish their crimes. For if some enemy who
openly tries to kill you deserves death or exile, what penalty
can be found to punish one who did the same as a friend,
under the cover of friendship? There is certainly none that I
know of. For if disdain or some particular circumstance leads
someone to try to kill you—openly and not through deceit,
such as an enemy moved to anger—he has shown you his
heart, and thus merits some excuse, since he has shown the way
and means for you to defend yourself and to do the same to
him. But this is not the case with a traitor, who acts with more
ease and attempts to harm you without any danger to himself,
and always from a point where you least expect danger. So I
believe that the worst vile traitors deserve the most atrocious
judicial punishments available. And if you desire your own
good and want to free yourselves of fear and danger, in my
judgment you should hang them all without mercy. In this way
we can securely bring order and rule to our well-being.

"Regarding this, I have thought that since there are more Assholes than Cunts or Cocks, we ought to make a fair and balanced distribution: This way we will all become equal and participate in all benefits. We should arrange ourselves so that each Cock is with an Asshole and each Cunt is with an Asshole. And in this way we might give the Assholes half of the state since both their distinguished actions and their greater number merit it. And the Cocks and Cunts will not be able to say that anything is lacking from their share. And since the Assholes will receive this benefit from us, I would like them to be seated apart, and thus they would be set behind both the Cocks, and us Cunts, keeping, however, their ancient dignities and privileges, with the condition and agreement that Cocks would have the same rights as regards Assholes and Cunts. Entry and exit in each case would be public and common, with the promise always to observe that which had been agreed on. In this way peace and union will be born between us, and it will give rise to infinite benefits. I humbly beg and urge you to do this."

And so it is that Cunts, like women greedy and eager for gain, always look with such fervor for Big Cocks, like a person who wants very badly to win a promised prize.

Why Women Long for Big Cocks

And so it is that Big Cocks are always represented with a rattle, or should I say "bell." They hated the bells so much and were so afraid that they lost themselves in woods and forests, and never dared to show themselves in any inhabited area where people could kill them or denounce them. They lived a bitter and savage life. Their fear was so great that they were never again seen by anyone in these parts, and so it came

Why Cocks Are Depicted with Rattles

to be widely believed that none would ever be found again. But in our own time a few have been found on the desert islands newly found at the other end of the world by the Portuguese fleet,[99] including the boat of Zena, our own Sienese (who transported bankrupts into those parts, for truly there is so much gold in those lands that every other thing seems lacking). They say the Cocks have all been transformed into other animals, and they have brought back quite a few pictures of them in various forms.

Why Cocks Are Depicted with Wings and Feet   You may have seen an example of this in our own university, or in that of Pisa or Padua, where on all the walls and benches Cocks are painted in varying fashions, and carved with wings, and feet, and beaks, and little hands, and other particular details. I think this was caused by new mixing of parts from various animals, as you may read about the Minotaur in Ovid, the Centaurs in Homer, and also the Pulicane in Bevis of Hampton.[100] But truly their shape is as I have described it, and it is certain that from here to the Pillars of Hercules[101] none can be found painted in any other shape, not even those who as a result of their dispersal and contrite devotion made themselves friars, but none are to be found among those twisted necks.[102]

The fate of the wretched Balls would have been much worse, if Cazzocchio and the aforementioned Cazzatello,[103] their old and dear friends, had not stuck their heads out and demanded a vote, and they cleverly spoke publicly in their favor: "Among the most beautiful and praiseworthy acts of justice the most highly esteemed are those that punish and absolve each person according to their merits. Thus it is that, thinking about the grave actions committed by those vile and brutal Balls, which led us into danger of perpetual enslavement, we believe that were we to kill them, we would do them a great wrong, when we intended only severe and dignified justice. Indeed, there is no punishment in the world as brief as death, and being brief, there can be no sadness after it, nor can any suffering or torment be felt. So it seems to me that, if we kill them all, we would be merciful and courteous to them—for they are worthy neither of torments nor of cruelty. On the other hand, so that you will be at peace, I believe that since their sin is inextinguishable, so their punishment should be unending, and we should condemn them to lasting death and eternal sorrow. Among all the punishments that come to my mind, I have fixed on one that is the worst that anyone could imagine, and which will be useful and serviceable to us. This is that we should lock them in sacks, two by two, and then distribute them—one pair between each Cock and Asshole, and also between each Cunt and Asshole, given that each Cock and Cunt will be paired with an Asshole, following the prudent counsel of the wise Cunt of Modena. Thus we will be as secure as can be; it will work against them, and we will see evidence of our revenge everyday, making them suffer a thousand exacting punishments. We Cocks can use them to rest our heads against, for weighing so much, they tend to dangle down. You Cunts can use them to cover any hole you may have that you want stuffed up. And so we can put them to good use, while they are damned to perpetual servitude and thus will suffer an eternal death and infinite pains. For I don't know any of you who has not experienced, in your own lives, how much it is better to die than to live in servitude."

"Besides the benefits we can expect from this plan," Cazzetto[104] added, "this way we will not have to dirty our hands with vile and impure blood, like that of the Balls. If we kill them, as we might as the result of a pact or agreement concluded between ourselves, there would be none left alive to bear witness against us. On the other hand, keeping them alive to serve us, as Cazzocchio has suggested, will allow us to get everything we can from them. There may well come a time when their death may be advantageous, and then we can kill them to our profit."

The pious thoughts of Cazzocchio and the subtle reasoning of Cazzetto greatly pleased the Cunts and Assholes, who hated the Balls above all. Thus to put the plan into effect, they quickly summoned all the Balls and placed them into sacks, so that there was no possibility of delay. First they gave a pair to each Cock, and then those few that remained were seized by the Cunts and stuffed into their holes, which—damaged by those cruel Big Cocks—went all the way into the asshole. And because these holes were so big, the sacks with Balls in them could not fill them completely.

Why Cunts Stink of Shit

And thus it is that all Cunts, besides the rotten smell from that fistula I told you about, also stink of shit. And if you put your nose up close to them and consider the smell, you will find it is marked by the scent of shit. And thus the Balls that are inside the cunt have ended up in the asshole.

Why Women Love to Be Buggered

So it is that women have so much pleasure when they are fucked up the ass, because they feel pleasure from the cock rubbing against the Balls as it rams in and out.

This is why women come more quickly when they are taken from behind, because they come more quickly the more their Balls are rubbed, stroked, and slapped between the cock and the cunt. But since there were not enough Balls for every cunt, many were left without them.

Why Women Come More Quickly when They Are Fucked in the Ass

And this is why some women are more masculine than others—those who don't have Balls are cool and calm, but those who have them always have fiery spirits, and are sure to revenge every injury done to them—they torture Cocks with their cunt and their asshole, and this makes them proud. Because some Cunts don't have Balls, some Cunts smell much worse than others—for not having that sack of Balls—which blocks the opening to the passage of the shit—it is necessary that, when the asshole is closed and the cunt open, the odor of shit comes through that opening and enters the cunt, and thus those Cunts smell more. However, Accorto Intronato[105] says that the smell of shit is very sweet, and that he likes only Cunts that smell very strongly in respect to that shit. And this hole is the reason that many women, almost all, let certain farts fall from their Cunts, which—not being shaped like a trumpet and not having an aperture that impedes them like the asshole does—lets them out so diffusely and softly that they're called puffballs.[106]

Why Some Women Are Bolder than Others

And for the reasons given above, it follows that the Balls, as traitors, are so hated by Cunts and Assholes that they will receive none of them, and there has never been an ass so kind and gentle or a cunt so large that it will let them in, although they are always eager to enter. But their hatred is as great as can be imagined, and it seems to grow every day.[107]

Why Balls Enter Neither in the Cunt Nor the Asshole

*Why the
Cunt Leaps
Forward
with Such
Passion
when It Is
Fucked*

And thus it is that we see Cunts jump so eagerly on Cocks, as if they want to grab the Balls and make them suffer for their ancient crime. And so those miserable creatures find themselves—as you see—suffering the torments and sorrows we know they suffer all day long.

After hearing the cruel sentence passed on the Balls, and having quickly and severely administered the punishment, as the Cocks had suggested, the assembly followed the counsel of the great Cunt of Modena and set about dividing up the Assholes pairing up each Cock and Cunt with an Asshole. And the Assholes were placed behind the Cocks and Cunts, as we see they still are today.

Feeling their honor was slighted, Old Culiseo came from among the Assholes, and demanded recompense for their indignity in the following manner:

"Since your high prudence and subtle understanding is not hidden from us, fathers and mothers, I will not weary myself in setting forth our shame, for I feel certain that each of you well knows how great your own shame would be if you were placed where we are. Since we have been placed there for the universal benefit and stability of our state, and since many consequences come from this, we are quite content to remain there. For when we see that you on your part will look on our sufferings with a just eye, and will be to us as we are to you, as far as the common good is concerned.

"I say this because, despite our natural sufferings and our unhappy position, we want to participate in all things with the Cunts, except giving birth. In exchange for our lowly position we want to stand by you Cunts in all circumstances, and help you in all your necessary functions. And every time any of you wants to be fucked, we will undertake to remain beneath you, to help and assist you, using any means we can. Furthermore, I've decided that we will be so close that there will be little more than the width of a card between us, so when you want us, your servants, in your need, help will be very close at hand. Also you will be able to make use of our room, for when you have your "visitor" or any other stranger in the house, so that when your big chamber is full, you will not have to send Cocks away to sleep out-of-doors. And thus we will be a refuge for you and certain and trusted help when you need it. And because we will be such close neighbors, if the cock plays any tricks or does anything pleasing in our house, it will be an easy thing for you to feel every little thing, and thus you can take the same pleasure we do. So for all these reasons you should not want to turn your back on this agreement, since for a brief displeasure you acquire so many advantages. And if that doesn't please you, just remember that the things we are condemned to put up with don't please us.

"You Cocks, on the other hand, which we have to have for company, we are your companions and not your servants. For with the first error of having the most vile place is joined that of appearing to be your slaves. And we want a guarantee that no cock can enter into the asshole that accompanies it, otherwise we'll arrange our affairs another way. If you promise this, you must keep your word, and if you cannot keep your promise, tell us, otherwise we will treat you as we know we will be treated by you. On the other hand, should you want us to be your companions and brothers, you must treat us as brothers and companions in the flesh."

These final words of the proud Culiseo were not very pleasing to the Cocks, and there was much whispering among them that they should not deprive themselves of so much pleasure and convenience as would come from making use of the asshole that was attached to them. Gathering together, they held a great and secret parliament, of which the Assholes were very suspicious, for they thought they would be betrayed.

Why the Asshole Is Kept Shut

For they never trusted the habits of the Cocks, and they suspected that the Cocks would agree together to break their agreements all at once, and break into their houses unexpectedly. And so it is that to this day all Assholes are closed and tightly shut, just as if they saw a cock nearby and doubting its good intentions, feared to be taken unexpectedly and to lose all their rights—and all the more when Cocks are openly turned toward them.

Why Man Clenches His Ass after He Has Pissed

This is why as soon as you have pissed the first thing you do is to squeeze your ass tight, thus causing wind to move within your tender guts. And because the asshole is afraid to open to shit in case a cock might try to come in, it waits until the cock is busy pissing and then sends everything out.

Why We Fart When We Piss

And so it is that many times when you're pissing you let out a fart, because the asshole senses that the Cock too busy pissing to do anything else, and so it squeezes itself, and as soon as it sees the cock piss, it opens. And if at some point a lot of wind gathers the strength to push itself out when the cock isn't pissing, then it forces itself out with a loud noise and report, so that the cock, frightened by the clamor, will not dare attack. And this is why we hear a noise when we fart. It is true that sometimes they come out silently; and everyone does this artfully and slyly, so that the cock is not aware of its opening. So that it cannot enter in, breaking all these pacts and agreements. For even though these pacts seemd very con-stricting to the Cocks that, ceding to the infinite prayers of the Cunts, they gave the Assholes what they wanted.

And this is why every time a cunt wants to be fucked, it first puts the ass underneath itself.

Why the Asshole Is Placed Beneath the Cunt

Sodo: You must pardon me, Arsiccio. I cannot keep quiet at this. Because it's not true that the ass is always underneath. From what I've learned in a little book called *La Cortigiana*,[108] there are infinite positions for fucking, and the ass is often on top.

Arsiccio: I agree, Sodo, and I will tell you why. First, you know that anyone who has made a thing can unmake it, without hurting anyone. And it is no wonder that the cunt and the asshole have chosen to break their ancient agreement. When one party or another is not content with an agreement, you can't even say the pact was broken. These postures are mod-ern things, discovered since Cocks, Cunts, and Assholes lost the power of speech and no longer control their own affairs.

But I am speaking of ancient things, and at that time there were other ways of doing things. Then you could fuck openly in public and it was highly praised. Since that time people caught fucking have been banned, thrown out, and

Why Man Does Not Like to Be Seen Fucking

persecuted. And so you see that today everyone who fucks tries to do it secretly, and in hiding.

Why We Kiss with the Tongue While Fucking

And some believe that this causes the kissing with the tongue that we do while fucking, because one tongue binds the other in order to ensure that things remain secret. But this is another subject, and if we wanted to talk of all the effects caused by the mutability of things we would need at least a week, for men's insatiable appetites have never ceased to explore new ways to please themselves. And this labor is especially seen in things relating to fucking: fucking cross-bow style, fucking with legs around the neck, fucking Turkish style, corkscrew style, and many other difficult and unnatural ways.[109] Leaving these aside, I tell you that the ancient pacts and agreements between the Cunts, Cocks, and Assholes are those I told you of, and from these—as we read in the Baptistry of the convent of San Francesco[110]—they have rarely strayed, and then only by necessity or some other extraordinary case. And you should realize that, however much they may have had their authority taken from them in other areas, nonetheless they retain the power to judge their own business with each other. And know too that the faith given by the Cunts to the Assholes is as strong today as it ever was, since all the pain of giving birth, however great it may be, is borne by the cunt itself. And no less have the Assholes failed in their promises, for they have always backed up the cunt and helped it when it makes copies of itself.

Indeed, it is because of the asshole that the cunt is as big as it is, because the asshole turns itself into a cunt. If this were not the case, the cunt would seem much tighter than it is. And you know this is true, because when Guasparuolo lamented that his wife La Cecca[111] had an enormous cunt, she was told by a neighboring woman that she should put a Papal Pear[112] up her ass, which, filling up her asshole, would make her pussy that much smaller. And she did this right away. Her husband, finding La Cecca's cunt to be tight, fucked her more often, until one day, whether because a fart blew it out, or for some other reason, the pear fell out, and her pussy returned to its enormous size. I was told that, when the husband found his wife with that pear, he asked her where it came from. La Cecca told him she had brought it to bed that night, so that she could eat it after fucking, for her comfort. Her husband took the pear and, saying he had more need of comfort than she did, began to eat it. La Cecca began to laugh. Guasparuolo, wanting to know why she was laughing, found out that the pear he was eating had been up his wife's ass for a month to make her cunt tighter, which made him want to puke his guts out. Later, thinking about what had happened, he told his wife that she shouldn't put a pear up her ass, but to leave everything to him, and he would find a better solution. And from that time forth, I've heard he always fucked La Cecca up the ass, and she took great pleasure from it. And thus it is for all women, because their assholes are really miniature pussies.

And that's why experienced women don't want to be fucked if it's not up the ass, because that way they grip the cock—and they're all hungry for cocks—on all sides, whereas if they are fucked from the front they only touch it on two sides, and worse, it all gets lost inside the body.

Why Women No Longer Want to Be Fucked in the Cunt Once They Have Been Fucked in the Ass

*Why
Women,
after Giving
Birth,
Cannot Shit
for Three
Days*
And this is why after giving birth most women can't shit for three or four days, because their ass has turned itself into a cunt, and it takes some time to turn itself back again. I've told you these things, Sodo, so that you would know why the balls never go into the ass when you fuck—which earlier tonight you did not know. And if some other time you want to know about the war of the Cunts or the collapse of the Cock—all of which occurred a long time ago, I'll tell you another time.

Sodo: I beg you, Arsiccio, finish up as soon as you can, because I'm very sleepy. I've never had so much trouble staying awake as in the last few minutes. Your chatter has begun to bore me.

Arsiccio: You're right, Sodo. But tell me, should we leave the Cocks, Cunts, and Assholes in their senate, so that they can't go to sleep as well?

Sodo: No, let's get them out quickly.

Arsiccio: No, no. You go off to bed now. Let's let them stay there; they may do some good thing tonight that will give us more to talk about tomorrow evening. Good night.

NOTES

1. Bizzarro [Bizarre] Intronato was the academic name of Marcello Landucci. Moscone [Big Fly] Intronato was the academic name of Giovan Francesco Franceschi. The names and pseudonyms of 1,351 of the Academy's members from the fifteenth to eighteenth centuries are recorded in the records of the Academy in the Biblioteca Comunale in Siena (Cod. Y, I, 7). The names and pseudonyms of the most prominent members are reprinted in Lolita Petracchi Constanti, *L'Accademia degli Intronati di Siena e una sua commedia* (Siena: Editrice d'Arte, 1928), 64–67.

2. As with the "dark lady" of Shakespeare's sonnets, it is unclear whether the "black" girl *(una certa sgraziatella neràcchiola)* is dark-haired or dark-skinned. Some Africans *were* kept as household slaves in Italy in the early sixteenth century—see Fernand Braudel, *The Mediterranean and the Mediterranean World in the Age of Philip II*, translated by Sian Reynolds (New York: Harper, 1973), 754–55.

3. Arsiccio [Burned] was the academic name used by Vignali himself. "Sodo," a name suggesting "sodomy," was the name used by Marcantonio Piccolomini, who also appears as an interlocutor in the 1572 *Dialogo de' giuochi* (Dialogue on Games) by the Sienese author Girolamo Bargagli.

4. Academy of the Intronati (The Academy of the Stunned), a confraternity of Sienese intellectuals, founded in 1525. Vignali was one of the six founding members. Members were registered in the Academy under comic pseudonyms, such as Vignali's "Arsiccio Intronato" (Burned Intronato). See Introduction, pp. 12–17.

5. *Decameron* 8.7. This tale tells the story of a scholar who is made to stand all night in the snow by a widow he is courting. In revenge he tricks her into standing naked all day on the top of a tower in midsummer, where she is exposed to the view of the city and tormented by heat and stinging insects. The tale is the longest in the *Decameron*, in part because of the lengthy speeches of the scholar berating the woman.

6. In fact, in the sixteenth century scholars were not particularly knowledgeable about contraceptives and abortificients. Information on such topics seems to have been transmitted largely as folklore, from mother to daughter. For a variety of reasons, including the Church's strong disapproval of nonprocreative sex, scholarly knowledge of such subjects had in fact declined greatly since the classical and early medieval periods. The

most common methods used seem to have been the oral ingestion of herbs such as pennyroyal and rue, and vaginal suppositories made from lilies or juniper berries. See John M. Riddle, *Contraception and Abortion from the Ancient World to the Renaissance* (Cambridge, Mass.: Harvard University Press, 1992).

7. Aqua fortis (nitric acid) is a strong solvent, whose use was common in alchemy.

8. Salavo—"Salty" Intronato—was the academic name of Giovan Battista Ornoldi.

9. This silly question, which provides the impetus for the whole dialogue, is reminiscent of the first of Aretino's sonetti lussuriosi (c. 1525) which ends "E s'e possibil fore / Non mi tener la potta I coglioni / D'ogni piacer fottuto testimoni" (And if it's possible, don't leave my balls outside your cunt, the witnesses of every pleasure).

10. Genesis 1.26–28; Ovid, *Metamorphoses* 1.76–88.

11. Tithones was a shepherd beloved by Aurora, goddess of the dawn. He was granted eternal life, but not eternal youth, and he was thus an iconic figure of decrepit old age.

12. This epithet "proud shaft" (*fiero scatapocchio*) is an odd word, deriving from "*batacchio*" (big stick). It is also found in a sonnet by the fifteenth-century erotic Florentine poet Burchiello: Burchiello del Bellincioni, *Sonetti del Burchiello del Bellincioni e d'altri poeti Fiorentini all Burchiellesca* (London, 1757), 86.

13. Genesis 1.28.

14. Aristotelian theories of conception postulated that male seed contained an active life-giving force that was shaped in the passive receptacle of the womb. Wasted sperm is thus wasted life force that has been deposited in an improper receptacle.

15. This is the curse of God on Onan: Genesis 38.9–10. Onan spills his seed on the ground rather than impregnate his brother's widow. In punishment for his refusal to continue the family line, God kills him.

16. See Matthew 3.10 and 7.19, as well as Luke 3.9.

17. Martial *Epigrams* 11.43: A poem in which a wife criticizes her sodomitical husband for buggering boys instead of her, since, after all, she has an anus too. He finally replies, "Parce tuis igitur dare mascula nomina rebus / teque puta cunnos, uxor, habere duos." ("Be content, therefore, to give your things a masculine name, and think, my wife, that you have two cunts"; lines 11–12).

18. Claudio Tolomei (1492–1555?), a prominent Sienese intellectual, especially active in debates over the status of the Italian language. He left Siena for Rome in 1518 and served both the Medici and the Farnese before becoming bishop of Corsola in 1549. As well as theoretical works on Italian language and poetics, he is thought to have written erotic verse which is now lost.

19. A manuscript copy of the first two stanzas of this sestina is in the Florentine National Library MS Palatino 256 (f. 208r), the same composite manuscript volume of Sienese verse that includes the only known copy of Vignali's poem "A la gratia." Tolomei's sestina is remarkable in that it exists in two versions—one polite, with lines ending in romantic words "lume, fiama, morta, voglia, cuore, volto" (light, flame, death, wish, heart, face), and another in which these terms are replaced with obscene ones: "pivo, nacia, potta, foia, cazzo, culo" (prick, thigh, buttocks, cunt, lust, cock, asshole).

20. "Musky" Intronato—a name not found in any of the Academy's records.

21. This passage vaguely evokes the myth of the hermaphrodite told by Aristophanes in Plato's *Symposium* (189b–193e). See also note 48, and Introduction, p. 32.

22. Claudio Tolomei—see note 18.

23. "Discreet" Intronato. Though the name appears in a list of members from 1654, no record is found of anyone using this name in the sixteenth century.

24. The heretical notion that Heaven, Hell, and Purgatory are to be understood not as actual places the soul would journey to after death but as metaphors for states of mind among the living was found among the Lollards, as well as later among the Familialists and other radical Protestant sects.

25. The following story has obvious parallels to the Fable of Menenius Agrippa (Livy, *Ad urbe condita* 2.32–2.33). See Introduction, p. 27.

26. In the sonnet "Son diventato in questa malattìa" (I have fallen into this sickness) (Burchiello, *Sonetti*, 100) defecation is described as "il far la cortesìa" (making courtesy), hence the notion that assholes must be courteous.

27. Penalties for those engaging in anal sex in Italy at this period were in fact extremely harsh. In Florence and Venice those convicted could be

burned alive, and though in practice the laws were enforced with some leniency, executions were not uncommon. On Venice see Guido Ruggiero, *The Boundaries of Eros: Sex Crime and Sexuality in Renaissance Venice* (New York: Oxford University Press, 1985), 109–145. On Florence see Michael Rocke, *Forbidden Friendships: Homosexuality and Male Culture in Renaissance Florence* (New York: Oxford University Press, 1996).

28. Some accounts of the founding of the Intronati claim that Vignali and several of his friends got the idea for their Academy while they were law students at the University of Pisa. The participants in this discussion have not been identified, however.

29. Coarse flax or hemp, prepared for spinning.

30. Sexual intercourse during pregnancy was frowned on by the Church, because even within marriage, sex was legitimate only if its goal was procreation. But, in print at least, there was not much open discussion of sexual positions and their implications for fertility. The Church's explicit denunciation of any position other than the "missionary" one with the man on top belongs largely to a later period.

31. The Catholic sacrament of Baptism included both the anointing of the baby's head with water and the placing of salt in the child's mouth. While generally retaining Baptism as a sacrament, the various Protestant sects approached the liturgy and ritual in many differing ways in the sixteenth century. There was controversy over whether salt should be used, and also over whether the ministrant should make the sign of the cross with the water.

32. In classical mythology, the Fortunate Isles are a paradise existing at the furthest bounds of human geographical knowledge. They were sometimes associated with the actual Canary Islands. The references to Homer, Pliny, and Socrates are all parodic—Arsiccio draws mockingly from a broad range of disciplines: poetry, natural history, and philosophy.

33. Python was a mythical serpent killed by the god Apollo at Delphi when it tried to prevent him from establishing an oracle there. The victory of Apollo, the sun god, over the serpent was often interpreted as a victory of the heavenly over the earthly. The references to Aristotle and the Greek geographer Strabo (c. 63 BCE–c. 23 CE) are again parodic, though it is fitting that Arsiccio should suggest that the penis was created from the slime of the great serpent.

34. These references, confused and parodic, refer to the emperor

Justinian's *Corpus of Civil Law*, a sixth-century compilation of all previous Roman law. The "Autentico" was a name sometimes given to the *Novels*, the section of the *Corpus* devoted to new laws written by Justinian himself. Bolognese scholars used the term "Digesto Vecchio" to refer to the first twenty-four books of the *Digest*, the section of the *Corpus* dealing with jurisprudence. The *Codex*, or *Codex Constitutionum* was the section of the *Corpus* compiling Imperial edicts.

35. The precise text is unknown, though similar texts from the period are not uncommon.

36. *The Golden Ass* 10.22

37. This story is taken from Poggio Bracciolini, *Facezie* 43.

38. Montalcino, a small hill town about twenty miles south of Siena.

39. Given that the engendering of legitimate children was the justification for the institution of marriage, such public trials of potency did in fact occur in the early modern period. See Pierre Darmon, *Trial by Impotence* (London: Chatto & Windus, 1985), who describes the phenomenon in six-teenth- to eighteenth-century France.

40. San Gimignano, a hill town about twenty miles northwest of Siena, is famous for its medieval towers, built by warring factions in the twelfth and thirteenth centuries.

41. Colle di Val d'Elsa, a town on the road between San Gimignano and Siena.

42. In classical mythology, Jove spent his childhood on Crete, hidden from his jealous father, Saturn.

43. A similar comparison between human and animal sexual habits is found in Macrobius's *Saturnalia* 2.5.10.

44. "Curly" Intronato—Alessandro Marzi, one of the six founding members of the Intronati. In 1571 some of his poetry and letters were published in the same volume as Vignali's "Lettera in proverbi." See Introduction, p. 59.

45. "Annoying" Intronato—Francesco Sozzi, another founding member of the Intronati.

46. "Hard" Intronato—the academic name of Andrea Landucci.

47. No member of this name is recorded. The Capponiano manuscript reads "Capercio," which would be Francesco Tedesco. But "Caperchia" could also be a scribal error for Cappochio—Orlando Malavolti.

48. "Secret" Intronato—another unknown academician.

49. Copies of this poem survive from the seventeenth century, including a Venetian dialect translation by Giorgio Baffo "Niove mistri s'ha messo a far la potta."

50. In Plato's *Symposium* 189b–193e, the playwright Aristophanes recounts a myth of human generation which posits that all human beings were originally hermaphroditic, until Zeus split them into two halves. Each half now wanders the earth seeking its other half, and this explains both sexual union and sexual preference: males whose other half was male will seek to join with other males; males whose other half was female will seek females, etc.

51. Bembo explicates the Platonic myth of the hermaphrodite in *Asolani* 2.11. There is no mention, however, of the following story.

52. Bizarro Intronato, Marcello Landuci, is the supposed author of the fictional letter introducing the dialogue. Pietro Bembo (1470–1547), the Venetian humanist and cardinal, was known for his idealized Platonic view of love, and left no writings dealing with the matters under discussion here.

53. A dabbudà is a stringed instrument resembling a psaltry, and not the name of a philosopher.

54. That is, "The Light of Shame," a parody of titles of devotional works such as *Lumen vitae*, "The Light of Life," or *Lumen animae*, "The Light of the Soul."

55. In Italy, as in the rest of Europe, there was great debate in the sixteenth century over whether serious writing should be in Latin or the vernacular. Machiavelli, Bembo, Castiglione, and Ariosto all chose Italian.

56. A proverbial way of saying a task is useless. The same expression occurs among the proverbs in Vignali's *Letter* (8) and also in *Gl'Ingannati* 3.1, where it is said to be so ancient its origin is unknown.

57. *Rime* 207, "che'n giovenil fallir e men vergogna" (in youthful failings there is less shame, line 13).

58. The words for traitor (*traditore*) and translator (*traduttore*) are very similar in Italian. While translation of various classical texts into the vernacular was a common practice before the sixteenth century, the invention of printing ensured that translated texts had an unprecedented circulation. Vignali is probably not entirely serious in his condemnation of the practice, given that one of the projects of the Intronati was to translate Latin

texts into Italian, and Vignali himself later produced a translation of books 11 and 12 of the *Aeneid* into Italian blank verse. None of these translations were published, however.

59. Pliny deals with the welding of iron in book 34 of his *Natural History*, especially sections 41 and 43.

60. Pliny, *Natural History*, book 2, sections 108 and 109, discusses various flammable liquids.

61. Macrobius discusses the flammability of oily seawater in *Saturnalia* 7, 13.24. Caius Julius Solinus deals with ways in which water reacts with burning vegetable oil in *Collectanea rerum memorabilium* 21.4.

62. The liberal arts, learned in universities, included grammar, logic, rhetoric, and related intellectual fields. Mechanic arts were those crafts and skills such as wood or metal working, which required physical effort.

63. The relation between Latin and Tuscan was much debated in the fifteenth century, as were their relative merits as literary languages. See Introduction, pp. 25–26. In his *Cesano*, written at the same time as *La Cazzaria*, but not published until 1555, the Sienese scholar Claudio Tolomei proves that Latin and Tuscan are indeed separate languages (see note 18).

64. Debates over the development and status of the Italian vernaculars often turned on the question of non-Latin terms introduced by Germanic invaders after the fall of the Western Empire in the fifth century.

65. Attempts to regularize vernacular Italian include Fortunio's *Regole grammaticali della volgar poesia* (1516) and Bembo's *Prose della volgar lingua* (1525), as well as Trissino's *L'Epistola delle lettere nuovamente aggiunte* (1524).

66. Tuscan was coming to be used as a literary language throughout Italy.

67. In *Prose della volgar lingua* Bembo refers to many of these same "new words," although most of them had been in use since the thirteenth century and were thus not very new. Bembo considers "sovente," "guari," and "altresì" to be provincial dialect (1.10), and discusses "unqua" and "mai" as negative participles (3.51).

68. Though Arsiccio enjoys making fun of Bembo, this concept of the harmonization of language follows Bembo quite closely.

69. This view was held by Cristofero Landino (1424–1504), a scholar associated with Ficino's Platonic Academy. See Cristofero Landino, *Scritti critici e teorici*, edited by R. Cardini (Rome, 1974), 38.

70. That is, the meter of Tuscan poetry is not qualitative as is that of Latin poetry.

71. Another theory of Landino's: Landino, *Scritti critici*, 34, 129.

72. The town of Belforte di Radicondoli, southwest of Siena.

73. Martial's epigrams, Ovid's *Ars Amatoria* and *Amores*, and Apuleius's prose satire *The Golden Ass* all deal with sexual issues quite explicitly. Horace is less explicit, but his satires, especially 1.2, are also bawdy. The reference to Virgil is probably to the *Priapea* attributed to him by Donatus and Servius, and included in the *Appendix Vergiliana*.

74. Doctor and naturalist who studied at the University of Padua at the beginning of the fourteenth century.

75. Both Tivizzano and Sosperone Intronato are not in the list of the Academy's members.

76. Another parodic reference: Ippocrates was a Greek medical authority: In Italian his name, "Ippocrate" closely resembles "Porco grasso" (fat pig). The pun appears already in the *Decameron* 8.9.37, and Vignali uses it again in *La Floria* (Act 3.5; sig. E2r). Needless to say, Ippocrates never wrote anything called *Palette* ("Spades"), let alone something six thousand verses long.

77. The quote "Without Ceres and Bacchus Venus grows cold" (Love grows cold without food and wine) is from Terence (*Eunuch* 4.5.6) not Ovid. The original text reads: "Sine Cerere et Libero friget Venus." Cicero quotes and explicates the phrase in *De natura deorum* 2.60.

78. This passage begins the allegory of contemporary Sienese politics that takes up most of the second half of the dialogue. Each group in Arsiccio's fable, the Cocks, Cunts, Assholes, and Balls corresponds to a particular faction in the city. See Introduction, pp. 33–34.

79. The Roman historian Livy (Titus Livius, c. 59/64 BCE–17 CE) wrote a massive history of Rome in 142 books, the earliest of which dealt with ancient history. While Livy provides Vignali with the Fable of the Body attributed to Menenius Agrippa (see note 25 and Introduction, p. 27) this is another parodic reference. The second *Decade* of Livy (books 11–20) was lost after the classical period.

80. On the specific identity of Cazzone—the Big Ugly Cock, who leads the dominant Monte dei Nove, see Introduction, pp. 34–35.

81. That is, for first prize.

82. Literally, make me an "intronato," a dolt.

83. An expression that refers to the way loaves of bread come out of an oven in different shapes.

84. A blasphemous pun on "Cunt of the Madonna." The phrase also occurs in *Gl'Ingannati* 3.1, where visitors to Modena include the "potta da Modana" in a list of local attractions.

85. The text is somewhat unclear at this point. Cugino ("Cousin") Intronato is not mentioned in the Academy's records. The Capponiano manuscript has Caggiano, also unknown.

86. Via San Martino is the main street of the San Martino district in southeast Siena.

87. Folletico "Elfin" Intronato—another unknown, though there was a Sollecito "Quick" Intronato (Giovanni Lucrezio) and a Falotico "Phallic" Intronato (Antonio del Diligente).

88. Affumicato "Smoked" Intronato—Achille d'Elci, an author of legal texts.

89. Svegliato "Wide-Awake" Intronato—a name that appears in the lists only after 1557, at which time it refers to Diomede Borghese. The name could also be an error for Svogliato "Lazy" Intronato (Lattanzio Tolomei).

90. "Shady" Intronato—Figliuccio Figliucci, bishop of Chiusi.

91. Vaguely orientalist nonsense. Beffania derives from "*Beffa*" ("fool"). Archifanfano is a nonsensical name that appears in comic plays as a parodic reference to a Muslim scholarly authority. Baldracca suggests Baldac (Bagdad) as well as the Baldracca, a Florentine hostel for "fallen women." Aldalecca is close to "*al di là*"—over there; "lecca" means "lick." Giudecca is an area of Venice, whose name reflects the fact that it was home to a Jewish community in the thirteenth century. The Yellow Sea is the sea between China and Korea.

92. Brother Buio—Brother Darkness, clearly not the name of an architect.

93. Scannaconfetti—another silly name. "*Scanna*" suggests "*scannare*"— "to butcher"; "confetti" are sugared almonds.

94. Impassionato "Impassioned" Intronato—unknown again, but the Capponiano manuscript has Impacciato "Embarrassed" (Tommaso Docci).

95. Cazzatello—little cock.

96. The division of possible forms of government into monarchy, oli-

garchy, and democracy is found in Plato's *Republic* I.338d.

97. The name of a coarse type of cloth.

98. Slang for mons veneris—see *Decameron* 6, introduction 8, where the expression is used by a lower-class woman.

99. The expedition of the Florentine Amerigo Vespucci, sailing under the patronage of the king of Portugal in 1501–1502, charted the Atlantic coast of South America. An account of the voyage, *Lettera delle isole nuovamente trovate*, was published in Florence in 1505, though it makes no mention of a Sienese captain called Zena.

100. All monsters combining human and animal physiognomy: The Minotaur had a bull's head and a man's body, see Ovid, *Metamorphoses* 8.152. Centaurs are traditionally half man and half horse, but Homer describes them as being a wild people of central Greece (*Iliad* 1.312). Pulicane is a creature with a human body and a dog's head who appears in the chivalric romances featuring the hero Bevis of Hampton, which were very popular in late medieval Italy.

101. The Pillars of Hercules are the ancient name for the straits of Gibraltar, which separate the Atlantic from the Mediterranean.

102. A common term for hypocrites: Friars were in the habit of bending their necks when praying.

103. Cazzochio "plump cock."

104. Possibly an error for "Cazatello"—both mean "little cock."

105. Accorto "Perceptive" Intronato—Don Giovanni di Luna.

106. Puffballs, that is, "*vesce*"—an Italian term for silent farts.

107. Finally the solution to Sodo's initial question. And it contradicts what Arsiccio has just said about some women having balls inside their vaginas.

108. The identity of this text is unclear, though it is not Aretino's comedy *La Cortigiana*, which has no such list. The text described may be the *Dialogo di Maddalena e Giulia*, sometimes known as *La Puttana errante*, an anonymous erotic dialogue sometimes attributed to Aretino that provides long lists of postures for sexual intercourse.

109. A similar list appears in *Dialogo di Maddalena e Giulia*, edited by Claudio Galdersi et al. (Rome: Salerno, 1987), 97–105.

110. Baptistry of the convent of San Francesco, a large Gothic church in Siena, built in 1326–1475 and gutted by fire in 1655.

III. A later version of this story is found in the ninth tale of the *Giornate delle novelle de' novizi* by the Sienese author Pietro Fortini (c. 1555) (2 vols. Adriana Mauriello, ed., Rome: Salerno, 1988) I.200–215. In that tale, a poor girl from Volterra who has been a bishop's concubine is married off to a local man, and her widowed mother suggests using the pear to conceal the fact that the girl is no longer a virgin.

112. A particularly large variety of pear.

Bibliography

Editions of *La Cazzaria*

Manuscripts

B   Badajoz, Spain, Biblioteca Publica, Barcarrota MS I. Sixteenth century.

C   Vatican Library MS Capponiano 140, ff. 1–77. Seventeenth century.

Early Editions

[N] Now lost: "ad istanza di Curzio e Scipione Navi" octavo, Naples 1530–1540?, 142 pages. Described in 1860 by the French bibliographer J. C. Brunet.

E   Paris, Bibliotèque Nationale, Enfer 566, octavo, Venice 1531?, ff. 91; ff. 1–6 damaged.

EI   Paris, Bibliotèque Nationale, Enfer 565, octavo, Venice 1531?, ff. 91.

Modern Editions

La Cazzaria, edited by E. Cléder. Cosmopoli (Brussels), 1863. Italian text.

La Cazzaria, Dialogue priapique de l'Arsiccio Intronato, edited by Alcide Bonneau. Paris: Lisieux, 1882. Italian text with a facing-page French translation.

La Cazzaria, edited by G. Vorberg and W. Stekel. Stuttgart: J. Putnam, 1924. German translation with postscript by Stekel, a Freudian psychoanalyst.

La Cazzaria, Dialogue Priapique de l'Arsiccio Intronato, écrit par Antonio Vignali. Paris: Le Cercle du Livre Précieux, 1960. French translation.

Die Cazzaria. Hamburg: Gala Verlagt, 1963. German translation.

La Cazzaria, edited by Pasquale Stoppelli and Nino Borsellino. Rome: Edizioni dell'Elephante, 1985. Italian text based on E and EI; extensive annotations. Reprinted 1990.

La Cazzaria, edited by Giovanni Ravasio and Klaus G. Renner. Munich: K. G. Renner, 1988. German translation.

La Cazzaria, Dialogue Priapique de l'Arsiccio Intronato, edited by Jean-Paul Rocher. Cognac: Le Temps qu'il fait, 1996. French translation.

La Cazzaria (La Carajería) Diálogo, edited by Guido M. Cappelli, Eliza Ruiz García, Francisco Rico. 2 vols. Mérida, Spain: Editora Regional de Extremadura, 1999. Italian text and Spanish translation of the Barcarrota MS, with facsimile and textual notes.

OTHER WORKS BY ANTONIO VIGNALI

Published Works

Alcune lettere amorose, una dell'Arsiccio Intronato, in proverbi, l'altre di Allesandro Marzi, Cirloso Intronato, con le risposte e con alcuni sonetti. Girolamo Pecori, ed. Siena: L. Bonnetti, 1571; reprinted Florence: Libreria editrice fiorentina, 1975.

La Floria. Florence: Giunti, 1560, 1567.

Unpublished Works

A la gratia. Biblioteca Nazionale Centrale di Firenze, MS Palatino 256 c.

L'Antiopea. Biblioteca Communale di Siena, MS Misc. H X 5; 2.

"Capitolo bernesco" beginning "Quanto più col cervel girando a torno." Biblioteca Communale di Siena, MS Misc. H X 5; 2.

Translation of *Aeneid* XI and XII. Milan: Archivo Storico Civico e Biblioteca Trivulziana, MS 1110.

Another copy of *Aeneid* XI. Biblioteca Nazionale Centrale di Firenze, MS Palatino 381.

Secondary Texts

Archivo di Stato di Siena. *Deliberazioni di Balìa*, 82.

Aretino, Pietro. *Aretino's Dialogues*. Raymond Rosenthal, trans. New York: Marsilio, 1994.

Bargagli, Girolamo. *Dialogo de giuchi che nelle vegghie sanesi si usano di fare*. P. D. Incalci, ed. Siena: Ermini, 1982.

Bargagli, Scipione, *Il Turamino, ovvero del parlare e dello scrivere sanese*. Luca Serianni, ed. Rome: Salerno, 1976.

Barkan, Leonard. *Transuming Passion: Ganymede and the Erotics of Humanism*. Stanford, Calif.: Stanford University Press, 1991.

Borghesi, S. Bichi. *Bibliografia degli scrittori sanese*. Biblioteca Communale di Siena, MS P. IV. II.

Borsellino, Nino. *Rozzi e Intronati: Esperienze e forme di teatro del "Decameron" al "Candelaio."* Rome: Bulzone, 1974.

Braudel, Fernand. *The Mediterranean and the Mediterranean World in the Age of Philip II*. Sian Reynolds, trans. New York: Harper, 1973.

Bullough, Geoffrey, ed. *Narrative and Dramatic Sources of Shakespeare*. Vol. 5, *The Roman Plays*. New York: Columbia University Press, 1964.

Buñuel, Luis. *My Last Sigh*. New York: Vintage, 1983.

Burchiello del Bellincioni. *Sonetti del Burchiello del Bellincioni e d'altri poeti Fiorentini all Burchiellesca*. London, 1757.

Burnet, J. C. *Manuel du librairie et de l'amateur des livres*, vol. I. Paris, 1860.

Cantagalli, Roberto. *La Guerra di Siena: 1552–1559*. Siena: Accademia degli Intronati, 1962.

Celse-Blanc, Mireille, ed. *Aurelia: Edition critique*. Centre Universitaire de Recherche sur la Renaissance Italienne, 9, 1981.

Constantini, Lolita Petracchi. *L'Accademia degli Intronati di Siena e una sua commedia*. Siena: Editrice d'Arte "La Diana," 1928.

Cozzo, Giuseppe. *I Codici Capponiani della Biblioteca Vaticana*. Rome: Tipografia Vaticana, 1897.

D'Addario, Arnaldo. *Il Problema Senese nella storia Italiana della prima metà del cinquecento*. Florence: Felice le Monnier, 1958.

Darmon, Pierre. *Trial by Impotence*. Paul Keegan, trans. London: Chatto & Windus, 1985.

Findlen, Paula. "Humanism, Politics, and Pornography in Renaissance Italy." In *The Invention of Pornography: Obscenity and the Origins of Modernity, 1500–1800*, Lynn Hunt, ed., pp. 49–108. New York: Zone, 1993.

Fortini, Pietro. *Giornate delle novelle de' novizi.* 1555. 2 vols. Adriana Mauriello, ed. Rome: Salerno, 1988.

Foucault, Michel. *The History of Sexuality.* Vol. 1, *An Introduction.* Robert Hurley, trans. New York: Vintage, 1978, 1980.

Frantz, David O. *Festum Voluptatis: A Study of Renaissance Erotica.* Columbus: Ohio State University Press, 1989.

Freccero, John. "Medusa and the Madonna of Forlì: Political Sexuality in Machiavelli." In *Machiavelli and the Discourse of Literature.* Albert Russell Ascoli and Victoria Kahn, eds., pp. 161–78. Ithaca, N.Y.: Cornell University Press, 1993.

Fryer, Peter. *Private Case—Public Scandal.* London: Secker & Warburg, 1966.

Galdersi, Claudio, et al., eds. *Dialogo di Maddalena e Giulia.* Rome: Salerno, 1987.

Gigli, Girolamo. *Diario sanese.* Siena, 1772.

Grendler, Paul F. *The Universities of the Italian Renaissance.* Baltimore: Johns Hopkins University Press, 2002.

Hicks, David L. "The Sienese State in the Renaissance." In *From the Renaissance to the Counter-Reformation: Essays in Honor of Garrett Mattingly.* Charles H. Carter, ed., pp. 75–94. New York: Random House, 1965.

Hoppe, Harry R. "John Wolfe, Printer and Publisher, 1579–1601." *The Library* 4. 14 (1933): 241–87.

Isaacs, Ann Katherine Chiancone. "Popolo e monti nella Siena del primo cinque-cento." *Rivista Storica Italiana* 82, 1–2 (1970): 32–80.

Kantorowicz, Ernst H. *The King's Two Bodies: A Study in Medieval Political Theology.* Princeton, N.J.: Princeton University Press, 1957.

Kearney, Patrick J. *The Private Case: An Annotated Bibliography of the Private Case Erotica Collection in the British (Museum) Library.* London: Jay Landesman, 1981.

Landino, Cristoforo. *Scritti critici e teorici.* R. Cardini, ed. Rome: Bulzoni, 1974.

Livy. *The History of Rome.* Ernest Rhys, ed., Rev. Canon Roberts, trans. Everyman's Library. New York: J. M. Dent, 1912.

Machiavelli, Niccolò. *The Discourses of Niccolò Machiavelli.* 2 vols. Leslie J. Walker, S.J., ed. and trans. London: Routledge, 1975.

———. *The Prince.* Robert M. Adams, trans. New York: W. W. Norton, 1977.

Maylender, Michele. *Storia delle accademie d'Italia.* 5 vols. Bologna: Lincio Cappelli, 1926.

Moulton, Ian Frederick. "Bawdy Politic: Renaissance Republicanism and the Discourse of Pricks." In *Opening the Borders: Inclusivity and Early Modern Studies, Essays in Honor of James V. Mirollo.* Peter C. Herman, ed., pp. 225–242. Newark: University of Delaware Press, 1999.

Nuti, Giuseppe Palmieri. *Storia di Siena dalle origine alle 1559.* Siena: Libreria dell'opera metropolitana, 1968.

Panciroli, Guido. *De Claris legibus interpretibus.* 1637, 1721. Farnborough, U.K.: Gregg International, 1968.

Riddle, John M. *Contraception and Abortion from the Ancient World to the Renaissance.* Cambridge, Mass.: Harvard University Press, 1992.

Rocke, Michael. *Forbidden Friendships: Homosexuality and Male Culture in Renaissance Florence.* New York: Oxford University Press, 1996.

Rowland, Ingrid D. *The Culture of the High Renaissance: Ancients and Moderns in Sixteenth-Century Rome.* New York: Cambridge University Press, 1998.

Ruggiero, Guido. *The Boundaries of Eros: Sex Crime and Sexuality in Renaissance Venice.* New York: Oxford University Press, 1985.

Samuels, Richard. "Benedetto Varchi, the *Accademia degli Infiammati,* and the Origins of the Italian Academic Movement." *Renaissance Quarterly* 29 (1976): 599–633.

Sidney, Sir Philip. *Sir Philip Sidney.* Katherine Duncan-Jones, ed. New York: Oxford University Press, 1989.

Stewart, Alan. *Close Readers: Humanism and Sodomy in Early Modern England.* Princeton, N.J.: Princeton University Press, 1997.

Ugurgieri-Azzolini, Isidoro. *Le pompe sanesi, o'vero relazione delli uomini, e donne illustri di Siena, e suo stato,* Part I. Pistoia, 1649.

Varchi, Benedetto. *L'Ercolano.* 2 vols. Maurizio Vitale, ed. Milan: Istituto Editoriale Cisalpino, 1979. Reprint of 1804 edition, Milan: Società Tipografica de' Classici Italiani.

Vasari, Giorgio. *Le opere di Giorgio Vasari.* 6 vols. G. Milanesi, ed. Florence: Sansoni, 1906, 1973.

Vespucci, Amerigo. *Lettera delle isole nuovamente trovate.* Florence, 1505.

Vignali, Antonio. *Alcune lettere amorose, una dell'Arsiccio Intronato, in proverbi, l'altro di Alessandro Marzi, Cirloso Intronato, con le risposte e con alcuni sonetti.* Gianpaolo Percori, ed. Florence: Libreria editrice fiorentina, 1975.

Vignali, Antonio. *La Floria.* Florence: Giunti, 1560.

Vitale, Maurizio. *La Questione della lingua.* Palermo: Palumbo, 1978.

The text of this book was composed in Centaur with Waters
Titling display face. Book design by Dutton & Sherman Design.